Nehasane Fire Observer

An Adirondack Woman's
Summer of '42

The author at her cabin at Partlow in 1942, a place she renamed Green Valley.

Nehasane Fire Observer

An Adirondack Woman's Summer of '42

Frances Boone Seaman

Nicholas K. Burns Publishing
Utica, New York

Nicholas K. Burns Publishing
130 Proctor Boulevard
Utica, New York 13501

First Edition

ISBN 0-9713069-6-6

Library of Congress Control Number: 2002110648

Photos from the author's collection and, as noted in captions, from the collection of the Adirondack Museum, Blue Mountain Lake, NY 12812.

Cover painting by the author (as described in the book), 1942. Scene from the fire tower on Mount Electra looking south, showing Rock Lake and the Stillwater of Beaver River Flow.

Book design by Brian L. McDowell
Cover design by Alyssa Krill

To Ruth Timm, who encouraged
and worked with me.

NEHASANE PARK

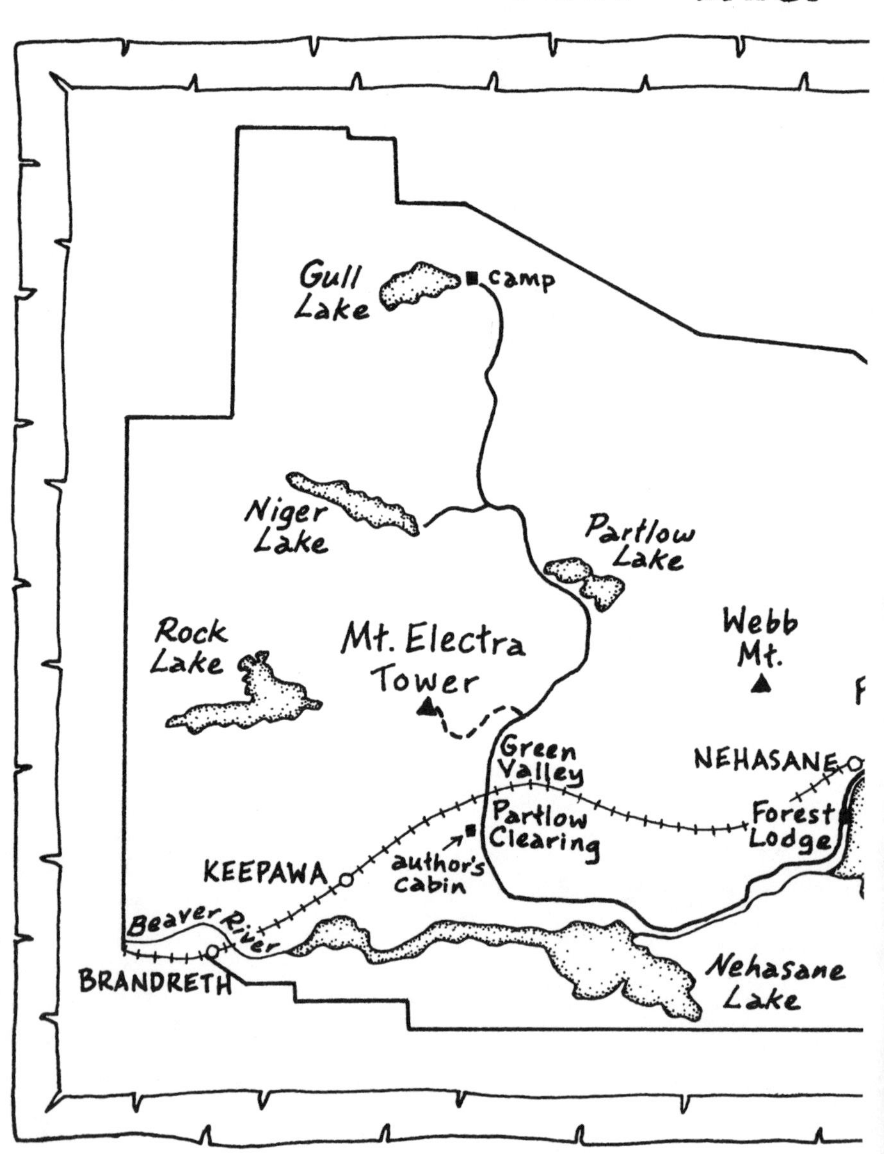

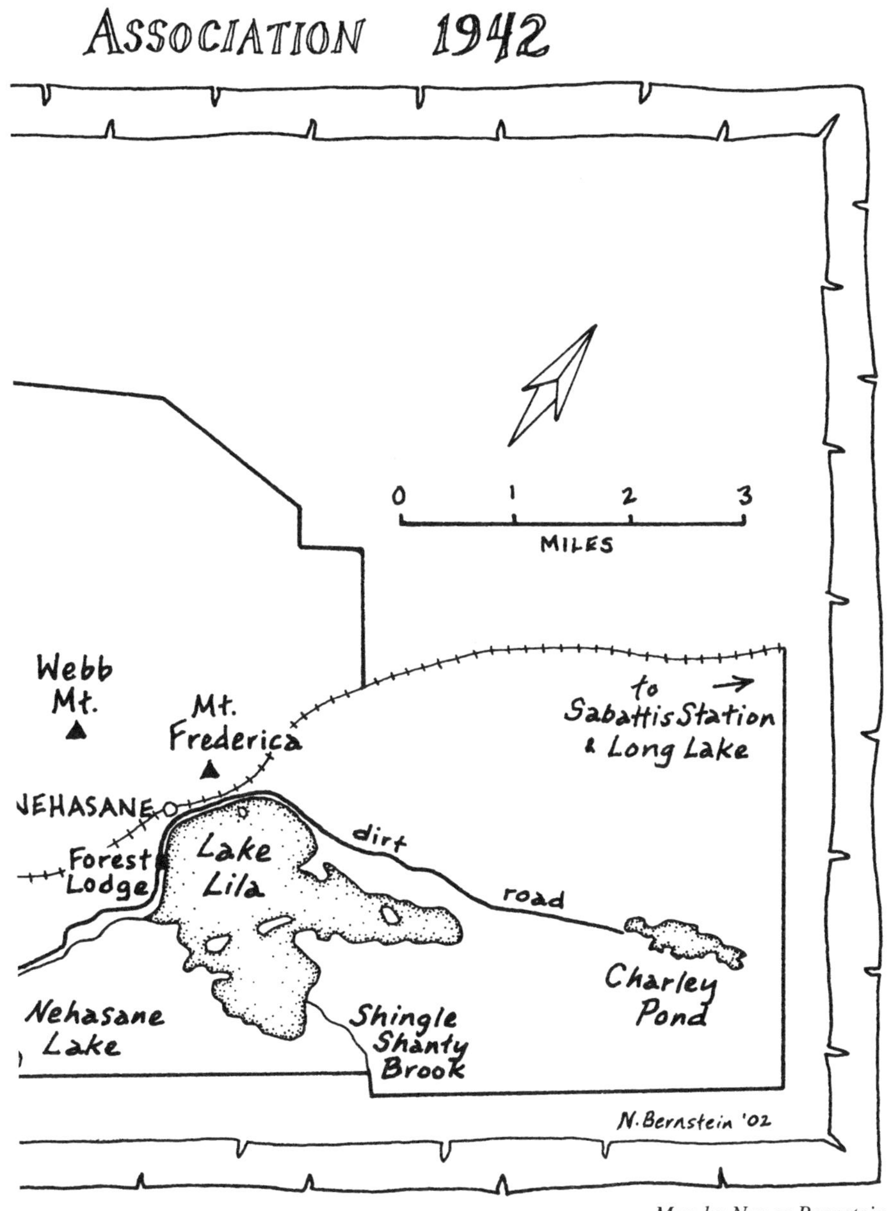

Map by Nancy Bernstein

Contents

Foreword

My quest to document the history and lore of the fire towers of New York State has taken me thousands of miles during the last four years. I discovered that during the early 1900s, forest fires raged across the state. Strong winds carried smoke and ashes that darkened the skies like an eclipse of the sun. People in mountain communities panicked, with many families forced to flee, clutching whatever valuables they could carry. Flames surrounded many of the towns and threatened homes and businesses. Every able-bodied man fought the fires alongside the fire wardens.

Many animals died during the fires, which usually occurred during the breeding season. Bushels of fish died in the streams from intense heat and from the lye that leached into the water.

In 1903, 643 fires ravaged 464,000 acres of land in the Adirondacks and Catskills. Again in 1908, fires engulfed the state's forests. There were 605 fires in the state and more than 368,000 acres burned with the cost of the valuable timber lost in the Adirondacks alone valued at $178,991. Many of the fires in 1908 developed along the New York Central, New York & Ottawa, and The Saranac & Lake Placid Railroads. Locomotives spewed sparks from their stacks and live coals flew from their ash pans onto the tinder-strewn right-of-way. Loggers left treetops, brush, and limbs to dry out near the railroad and surrounding woods, ready fuel for a fire.

The great fires of 1908 resulted in strong public demand for protection. The forestry industry and the big camp owners were alarmed while the thought of losing hunters and vacationers who brought money to the economy caused concern in the mountain communities. Flooding was a fear because with the destruction of the forests, there would be no vegetation to hold back the soil. Residents of cities outside the Adirondacks were concerned about the loss of clean water for drinking.

The state decided to adopt a program similar to one that Maine had been successful with since 1905. Under new laws passed in the spring of 1909, a more professional system of fire patrols charged not only with fire prevention, but game protection as well, replaced the fire wardens. Other changes included the introduction of fire observation towers, regulations on the railroads and the logging industry, and empowering the governor to close the forests if necessary.

In 1909, William G. Howard of the FFGC placed a high priority on the building of observation stations where fire observers could see smoke quickly over a wide expanse of forest. In 1909, fourteen observation stations began operation in the Adirondacks.

The observers worked from the first of April until the end of October. Most forest fires occurred during two times of the year. The first fire season was early spring, from the time the snow was gone and there were large amounts of dried leaves and grass, until the new foliage came out at the end of May. The second began with cold weather in September or October and ended with fall rains and snow. Periods of drought could extend the time of severe fire.

Large private landowners in the Adirondacks, such as C. V. Whitney and J. Watson Webb, were also concerned with protecting their thousands of acres of valuable timber. They hired patrolmen, and the Webb family even had its own fire fighting train and equipment.

The tower that Frances Boone Seaman observed from was a steel fire tower built on Rock Mountain (2,400 feet) in 1920. The mountain was renamed Mount Electra after Electra Havermeyer, the wife of J. Watson Webb.

The observers on Mount Electra were on the tower from late May or June until October. They worked seven days a week and were on duty at the tower from 9 A.M. TO 5 P.M. When it rained or if the forest was wet, the observer had the day off. The Webbs paid the salary, $90.20 a month, for one month and the state paid the remaining three months. Starting in 1934, the state used federal money from the Clarke-McNary Fire Fund to pay the observer.

The state has since purchased part of the Webb estate and retired Long Lake Forest Ranger Bruce Coon said that on September 25, 1989, he and Stillwater Forest Ranger Terry Perkins began dismantling the tower. The tower site is difficult to get to now because of the blow down of 1995.

Now, let's go back in time to the summer of 1942 when the tower is very much there. As we read Frances Seaman's memoir of her experience as the Nehasane Park fire observer, imagine that you are perched atop a 70-foot tower gazing at this huge expanse of trees and lakes. Feel the breeze against your face and drink in the spectacular Adirondacks. Now enjoy this beautifully written adventure and learn from Mrs. Seaman's first-hand account what it was really like to be a fire observer in the Adirondacks.

Martin Podskoch

Author of *Fire Towers of the Catskills: Their History and Lore.* Purple Mountain Press (2000).
His next book, *Adirondack Fire Towers: Their History and Lore* will be published by Purple Mountain Press in 2003.

Acknowledgments

First and foremost, I thank the Hamilton County Historical Society for its early and enthusiastic support. President Ermina Pincombe, as well as members Dr. Barbara Schoonmaker and Margaret Perkins, encouraged me to seek publication of my story. So, too, did another Society member, Adirondack historian Warder H. Cadbury. It was he who recommended the services of Ted Comstock, an editor whose in-depth familiarity with regional history proved to be a big help. Warder and Ted agreed that my manuscript had potential, but needed some "repairs" before it could see publication. A "mini-grant" from the Society enabled Ted to begin his editorial work. This grant was a timely financial boost for which I am grateful.

Margaret Perkins introduced me to Marty Podskoch of Delhi, N.Y., the author of *Fire Towers of the Catskills: Their History and Lore*. Marty, I learned, was researching the history of Adirondack towers for a forthcoming book. When he and his friend Bill Starr interviewed me, they generously shared what they knew about the tower on Mount Electra at Nehasane Park.

For technical support, I am indebted to Debbie Hall for typing my first draft, to my son John Seaman for the long hours he spent with a revised draft, and to Henning Pape-Santos of Ithaca, N.Y., for his prompt and expert word processing. Bruce Coon, New York State Forest Ranger, also offered advice and comment.

For many of the photographs in this book, I thank the Adirondack Museum and Jim Meehan, Manager of Historic Photographs. For his copy photography, I thank Jim Swedberg. Thanks also to Nancy Bernstein who contributed the map of the part of Nehasane Park that I came to know so well.

Finally, I thank my family and friends who believed from the start that the story of the summer I spent in an Adirondack fire tower sixty years ago was worth telling.

— One —

Getting Acquainted

I first visited Nehasane Park, an isolated private preserve near the center of the Adirondack Park, in the spring of 1940. I was twenty-one years old and had accepted a job as a waitress at Forest Lodge on Lake Lila, the camp of J. Watson Webb and his family of New York City and Shelburne, Vermont.

I remember the day well. It seemed as though I had been traveling most of it to get there. Actually, the forty-one-mile trip was the long way around. My home in Long Lake was less than twenty miles away, as the crow flies, from Lake Lila. After saying goodbye to my mother, I departed with my dad for the extended car ride to the train station at Sabattis. A small hamlet in the forest, the settlement consisted of several residences, a post office, a small school, a lumber company store, a boarding house, and the station.

When purchasing my ticket, I had to show my pass, the card that gave me permission to leave the train at Nehasane, the Webb family's private stop. My dad wished me well as I boarded and headed south. I really enjoyed the ride, as it was a novelty to me. My family lived too far from the railroad to use that mode of travel. The train halted briefly at Robinwood Station, the first stop below Sabattis. Presently, we were on our way again. We passed ponds and wetlands, lush and green in the spring sunshine, but I kept wondering what Nehasane would be like. The prospect of working for such wealthy people as the Webbs fascinated me.

The trip seemed to be taking a long time and I was getting more restless by the minute. Finally, I asked the conductor, "How much farther is it to Nehasane?"

"Next stop. You'll hear the whistle blow."

In a few minutes I did, and I prepared to get off. After alighting at the station, I noticed that there was only the one building, the station agent's office and home in the small clearing in the forest. Out of a nearby pickup truck stepped a gray-haired, neatly dressed man who introduced himself as George Collier, the superintendent of Nehasane Park.

"You're Frances Boone, I presume?" he asked.

"Yes, and I'm glad to meet you, sir," I replied, and added that it was a beautiful day for a train ride.

"You've had a lot of riding to get here from Long Lake," Mr. Collier said.

"Is Mrs. Virgil still cooking at the lodge?" I asked, since I had known her in Long Lake.

"Yes, she'll be glad to see you. I hope you won't mind riding in the truck?"

"Oh, no. It's part of the adventure."

After putting my luggage in the back, Mr. Collier suggested that I meet Mr. and Mrs. Wood, the station agents, before we departed. We walked across the yard to the office, and he introduced me to Pete Wood, station agent as well as postmaster. Pete was partially paralyzed from polio and had difficulty in getting around, yet as I later learned, he was a good-natured fellow who never complained. His wife Rose was a short, comely woman and I sensed right away that she liked to visit.

When we arrived at Forest Lodge on the shore of the lake, Mrs. Virgil was waiting for us. It had been several years since I had seen her, but she still had the ruddy complexion and ready smile that I remembered. Her brown hair had started to gray, and piled becomingly high on her head, it complimented her large frame.

"Say, Frances, it's great to see you again," she called out.

"I'm glad you're here. You make me feel right at home." I recalled our pleasant conversations when we'd meet at the store in Long Lake. We visited a few minutes and then she showed me to my room upstairs. The east end of the building contained the help's quarters. In addition to bedrooms, it had a spacious kitchen and dining area adjacent to a comfortable men's lounge on the side toward the lake. Beyond the kitchen was the laundry and cooler with its big icebox. The woodshed and the coal bin were in an annex at the back of the lodge.

I had experience working as a waitress at a Long Lake hotel and had handled the job deftly. It was good work for me, being a single girl looking for some excitement in my life and in need of a little extra money. Here at Forest Lodge it would be different, though, because I would be working for only one family. At first, I was a bit nervous about serving the Webb's and their elite guests, but the hospitable manner of Mr. Webb's fishing parties soon put me at ease. It wasn't long before we were exchanging casual greetings. I guessed that while here in the Adirondacks, they were able to let down their guard and relax just a bit.

Nehasane Park fascinated me from the very first day. To me it was a paradise enjoyed by these exciting people from a world very different from mine. Dirt roads were everywhere, leading through the woods to smaller outlying camps of the family members. Some were beside lakes and ponds. These people had so much access to fun here in the Adirondacks.

I was also intrigued when I heard about the fire tower on a mountain in the park. The main attraction at first was Forest Lodge, a handsome shingle-style building constructed on the south shore of Lake Lila in 1893. Facing north, it offered remarkable views out over the lake with its picturesque islands. Mr. Collier showed me around the complex a few days after my arrival. There were extensive quarters for the Webb family and their guests. For their use, there was a separate kitchen and two dining rooms, the smaller of which was for informal meals. Upstairs pleasant bedrooms faced the lake.

"I can't imagine anyone not being happy here, can you?" I said.

"It would have to be someone who didn't like the woods," he replied, and added, "The single gents who come as guests stay at the smaller lodge we passed back toward the station."

The layout of Forest Lodge had been well planned and was the design of Robert Robertson, a prominent New York architect. A spectacular room dominated the west end. The first time I entered, I looked around in amazement. The room was two stories high, and at one end, a fieldstone fireplace reached to the ceiling. On a ledge, looking at home in this rugged setting, a mounted full-grown panther (as they are known locally) looked down at us.

Mr. Collier could see I was impressed. He said, "This is one of the last panthers killed in the Adirondacks, all of fifty years ago." When I found my voice, I blurted out, "I wouldn't want to meet up with one of those creatures, but it sure looks great up there." I thought the rest of the room no less fascinating. Everywhere I looked, there were beautifully mounted animals and birds. From the ceiling, more birds hung in natural poses. Some were birds of prey, looking like they were about to swoop down to catch a meal. The heads of big-game animals, trophies, I assumed, from hunting expeditions around the world, covered the walls. I also admired the Indian artifacts from the American West. There were fringed and beaded articles of clothing and a number of Navajo rugs. I turned to Mr. Collier and exclaimed, "What a unique room! It's a real wildlife museum."

Realizing I was interested in the history of the park, Mr. Collier told me that a small hotel once stood on the shore of Lake Lila.

"Do you know where it was?" I asked.

Mr. Collier nodded. "It was right here where Dr. William Seward Webb chose to build this lodge."

"Oh," I said, "maybe this is also where David Smith built his hut when he came here from Long Lake in the 1840s."

"Perhaps Smith's clearing was still visible when that hotel was built," remarked Mr. Collier.

A few days later when I served Mr. Webb his breakfast, I asked him about the early times at Nehasane. He was usually reserved when it came to speaking with the help, so I was pleased that he was willing to fill me in with a little family history. He seemed very proud of it.

"My father was Dr. William Seward Webb. He was the president of the Wagner Palace Car Company, a railroad enterprise, and the son-in-law of William Vanderbilt. He purchased thousands of acres surrounding this lake, then known as Smith's Lake. He renamed it Lake Lila after my mother, Lila Osgood Vanderbilt."

I said, "Please go on. Did he have something to do with the railroad, too?"

"His interest in railroads led him to invest in building this railroad, the first to run through the newly established Adirondack Park. It began at Herkimer, east of Utica, and ran northward through the western Adirondacks. Eventually, the tracks were laid to Malone on the state's northern border."

"When did the Adirondack line connect with the New York Central?" I asked.

"Originally, the Adirondack line was called the Mohawk and Malone railroad. I don't recall the year that the extension of the tracks from Herkimer to Utica took place. It did improve train service, however." With that statement, my history lesson ended. Mr. Webb abruptly got up from the table and went in search of his guests.

On one of my first days off, when the Webb family and their guests had left for the day, Mrs. Virgil and Mr. Collier organized a picnic for the help on the summit of Smith's Mountain, a peak that Webb had renamed Mount Frederica after his daughter. Open and free of large trees at the top, the mountain was northwest of the lodge, not far from Lake Lila.

While Mrs. Virgil and Mr. Collier put together the picnic lunch, I took charge of the chores in the kitchen and made the beds. When all was ready, we met outside near the truck. Everyone was in good spirits, for the morning was sunny and clear. Besides Mr. Collier and Mrs. Virgil, we were joined by Tuffy, a kindly older fellow in charge of roadwork, and Harold, head of maintenance. There were also two acquaintances from Long Lake, Howard Seaman and Aldis Lamos, handymen at the lodge. Both were in their mid-twenties.

Into the truck went the lunches, bottled drinks, and a jug of lemonade that Mrs. Virgil had prepared. Mr. Collier invited her and me to ride to the start of the trail. The others walked. When they caught up with us, the fellows willingly accepted what they were asked to carry, but they wouldn't promise not to sample the chocolate cake that Mrs. Virgil had made the day before. As we hiked, the trail gradually became steeper. With the sun at our backs, I soon took my jacket off and the others did, too. I dropped back and climbed with Mrs. Virgil and Mr. Collier and, being thirsty, I asked for a drink of the lemonade.

"Oh, that tastes good!" I exclaimed, and the others heard me. They, too, stopped and wanted a drink, and the few minutes of rest revived us all. The winding trail, ever upward, gave no hint of the scenery below. A few minutes later, someone up ahead accidentally kicked aside a rock on the trail. Without warning, it started rolling down the path.

"Watch out!" Tuffy yelled. I looked up to see a rock the size of a football headed directly for me. I gasped and jumped aside as it bounded past. Mr. Collier and Mrs. Virgil were both in its path and it was gathering speed. He quickly pushed her aside, and leaped in the other direction. The rock disappeared down the trail. This happened so fast that Mrs. Virgil, who had landed on her side, luckily wasn't hurt.

"Sorry to upset you," Mr. Collier said as he helped her to her feet.

"If you hadn't," she panted, "I would. . . have been. . . hurt. Thank you," she said when she got her breath back.

An apology came down to us from one of the fellows up ahead.

Mr. Collier scowled as he glanced up at them.

"Better be more careful," he called out. "This is meant to be a picnic, not cause for an ambulance call."

Not until we came out of the woods near the summit were we rewarded with the view. Open places on the bare rock, alternating with clumps of low shrubs, made us pick our way carefully. Finally, we found a wide area of rock, and gathered to admire the scenery. Far below, Lake Lila reflected the blue sky, and the sun shining on the lovely bays and islands made the view well worth the climb.

"I could sit here all day and drink this in," Mrs. Virgil exclaimed.

"If we don't get any dinner, then we'll know where to find you," Mr. Collier replied.

As I looked to the east, Howard and Aldis vied with me to pick out Blue Mountain and Owls Head Mountain near Long Lake. Far to the northeast, we also made out the High Peaks north of Newcomb.

I asked Mr. Collier if we could see the fire tower from this vantage point.

"No," he explained, "the tower is about four miles south of here, and Webb Mountain is in our line of sight."

"What is the view like from the tower?"

"It's great. The tower room is well above the trees," he said. I could picture it, as I had once climbed the fire tower on Owls Head.

"Oh, wouldn't I like to climb that moun . . . . " My voice trailed off as I noticed Mrs. Virgil and Aldis starting to open the packs of food.

As we sat eating our lunch, I became better acquainted with Howard and Aldis. Howard was tall and athletic looking as well as quiet. Neither he nor Aldis smoked, which was unusual in those times. Both were from Long Lake. I had seen them around the village, but we were only casual acquaintances. Aldis may have been a little younger than Howard, but they had been friends since their school years. Aldis had a ruddy complexion and liked to joke and tease.

Although we were on the top of the mountain, black flies and a few yellow jackets pestered us, but we had a lively time, with lots of jokes and laughter. Howard kept an eye on the chocolate cake, as did Harold and Mr. Collier. After Mrs. Virgil finally cut and served it, everyone came back for more.

Back at the lodge on the following day, I found that I had an "axe to grind" with one of my new friends. In the dining room after helping Mrs. Virgil get the meal ready, I was "rewarded" with a surprise. The table was large and rectangular and covered with a patterned oilcloth that hung over the edges several inches. Everyone sat down with Howard between Aldis and me. After our plates were filled, we started eating. Suddenly I felt cold water running into my lap and I let out a yell. Aldis, I discovered, had played a trick on me. He had made a trough of the loose oilcloth in front of him and poured water along it, in front of Howard, into my lap! If Howard was aware of it, he didn't let on. Aldis grinned and Howard tried not to laugh. I jumped up, grabbed my glass of water and let Aldis have it—all over his head.

Mr. Collier looked shocked, but Mrs. Virgil managed to suppress a guffaw. For a minute, I was upset, then everyone began laughing, and I went to change my apron. Aldis found a towel and then excused himself to go put on a dry shirt. Mr. Collier soon regained his composure and sternly told the fellows to "cut out the tricks." Every meal after that I kept an eye on the tablecloth.

One Sunday afternoon, Howard asked me if I would like to go for a walk with him. He wanted to have a look at the old sawmill down the road toward Nehasane Lake. He didn't come out and say it, but I assumed that he also wanted to spend some time with me. Old machinery interested him, I later learned. The pesky black flies followed us everywhere and I was annoyed to think we'd forgotten the fly dope, so I broke off a leafy branch and used it as a switch to keep the flies away.

After looking over the mill, we noticed that the sky had turned dark. Then it started to rain and we ran along the road, hoping to get back to the lodge before we got soaked. It wasn't to be. Rain came in torrents. My hair was drenched and I could feel the water running down my neck. Howard's wet shirt stuck to his shoulders and water squished out of our shoes. As we ran, we kept splashing each other through the puddles. What would Mr. Collier and Mrs. Virgil say when they caught sight of us? By the time we reached the lodge, we were a sorry looking pair but nobody saw us come in. That day was the beginning of a beautiful friendship. Howard was special and I found that I liked him very much.

A week later, in the middle of June, my job as waitress ended. The guests' and Mr. Webb's fishing vacations had ended, and the rest of the Webb family would soon be arriving for the summer with their own staff. I made plans to return to Long Lake.

Months earlier, I had applied for the position of girl's camp councilor at Bob and Elvira Beatty's Caedmuir Lodge diagonally across the lake from the town dock. I was well versed in woodcraft, having studied Ernest Thompson Seton's woodcraft stories as a girl. Growing up I had spent a lot of time outdoors and had learned to hunt and fish as a teenager. I looked forward to teaching the younger girls what I knew. With all the fun and excitement of camp life, it was a pleasure to work at Caedmuir Lodge, and the Beattys later asked me to return as a councilor for the second summer.

When the time came to leave Nehasane, I reluctantly said good-bye to my new friends.

"Write to me," Mrs. Virgil pleaded. "It gets awfully lonesome here and a letter would cheer me up." Then Aldis chimed in, "How about writing to us? After you leave, we'll need cheering up too." Howard added, "You're taking away our sunshine." Embarrassed, I gave them both a scornful look.

Mr. Collier drove up to the porch to pick up my bags. Howard placed my luggage in the back of the truck and said, "I'll look you up when I get back to Long Lake." I glanced at his tanned face, and noticed he was smiling. I wondered if he really meant it. I hoped he did, and called out as I climbed in, "I'll be looking for you."

In the fall of 1940, I attended my first year of classes at the Albright Art Institute in Buffalo. Late in December, I had come home for Christmas vacation. Now it was the last day of the month and I was returning to Buffalo by train from Sabattis. I had hopes of seeing Howard again at the Nehasane Station.

The weather was very cold and there was well over a foot of snow on the ground. As the train neared the station, I heard the whistle announce the stop. Howard was still working at Forest Lodge, kept busy plowing snow. He knew I would be on this train, for we had talked a couple days before by telephone. The train would stop only long enough to pick up the mail.

As it came to a halt, I saw Pete and Rose Wood standing in the doorway of the station. I waved. They saw me and waved back. Then there was Howard walking alongside the train, looking for me in the windows above him. I caught sight of him and waved excitedly. He spotted me and pulled a camera from his pocket. To my surprise, he took my picture as I sat on the edge of my seat, peering out. Then he said something that I could not hear, but his grin pleased me. The train lurched and moved forward and I threw him a couple kisses. Nehasane soon became just a pleasant memory.

In December 1941, America entered World War II when Japan bombed Pearl Harbor. As so many young men did, Howard joined the armed services. He volunteered and signed up with the Air Force. Before he left for Fort Dix, he and Jim Emerson, a Long Lake friend, drove out to Buffalo to say good-bye. Howard promised to write me but none of us at that time knew when or if we would see each other again.

— Two —

My Cabin in the Backcountry

In the spring of 1942, I returned to Long Lake for Easter vacation. During the winter, I had continued my studies at the art institute in Buffalo. The war was on in Europe and nearly every day reports came in of planes, ships, and men lost in battle. It was depressing at times, but I tried to be optimistic. I had been hearing from Howard regularly while he trained as a mechanic at Langley Field in Virginia.

While at home, I received a letter from Mr. Collier at Nehasane Park. I wondered, when I first saw it, if they needed me again to help out in the dining room, but when I opened it I discovered that Mr. Collier had a different offer: Would I like to be the observer at the fire tower on Mount Electra this coming summer? I was elated. A job like that would be outdoor work. I'd be close to the natural world, and I felt sure there never would be a boring moment. Besides, I would be working for the State and, given the war, that was a reassuring thought. But when I showed the letter to my parents, they voiced concern. To them, Nehasane Park was an unknown. Never having been there, they envisioned all sorts of dangers.

"What if you fell or got hurt when you are alone?" my dad asked.

"Could you outrun a bear?" my mother wanted to know.

"I don't think anything will happen that I can't handle," I replied. "Besides, I know the people at Nehasane quite well, and that means a lot."

"How about strangers showing up unexpectedly?" my dad persisted.

"Because it's wartime, I don't think I will be bothered by anyone," I assured him.

"How about a telephone? Will you have one at the cabin?" my mother asked.

"Yes, and I think there are two at the tower. I'll have my bicycle to ride, as it's quite a distance from the cabin to where the trail starts." This I had learned from having talked with Howard and Aldis one day when they came in from working on the road. I also pointed out another factor in my favor: Nehasane was a private preserve.

My dad, a former homesteader in Oregon and no stranger to adventure, relented first. "As long as you're sure you can handle it, I guess it will be all right. What do you think, Mother?"

"I don't know," she replied, and I sensed her concern. "It seems like a strange place for a young woman to work. I want to think it over."

My day stalled right then. I tried desperately to keep busy, but the hours dragged on slowly. I helped my mother with the evening meal, but found it hard to keep up a conversation. When it came time to do the dishes, I plunged in with a will. That made me feel better and then I realized I had to be patient, for I sensed that she needed to talk the situation over with my dad. That night I slept fitfully. In the morning, I could only hope that the Lord had heard my prayers. To my relief, my mother consented. "Remember," she told me, "when you make an important decision, be prepared to stick with it."

I was overjoyed, and called Mr. Collier to accept and told him that this was what I wanted to do more than anything else that summer. He seemed pleased and relieved, adding that a reliable person for the tower job was hard to find. He said that I would start the first weekend of June.

During my last semester in Buffalo, my thoughts often returned to Nehasane Park. I thought fondly of my friendship with the boys, Mrs. Virgil's wholesome meals, and the satisfaction I had had working as a waitress. I recalled past conversations with Mr. Collier. He had shown me on a map the other large preserves bordering the Webb lands. C. V. Whitney owned land to the north and the Brandreth family to the south. I had heard of sections of virgin timber in large preserves in the Adirondacks and I knew that most of the owners had been good stewards.

Loss by fire of the valuable timber on these lands was often a possibility, particularly during the summer. It was the concern not only of the park owners, but also of the State. I was reassured in the knowledge that a network of mountaintop observers protected most of the Adirondack Park, on both public and private lands.

After I left Buffalo, I immediately prepared for my duties as fire observer. I organized all the items needed for my stay of four months in the interior of Nehasane Park. I was happy, caught up in the excitement of it all, yet still a little anxious. At one time, I would have been hesitant to take this job. Being a fire observer was considered man's work and I was concerned about what people would think of me. However, I wanted this job badly and the privacy and remoteness of Nehasane gave me the courage to go ahead. After all, not many people would know that a girl was the fire observer on Mount Electra.

Because the park had been in private hands for decades, wildlife abounded. Knowing this, my family and friends not only cautioned me of the dangers of a solitary life, but also tried to persuade me to take along a gun for protection. I decided my rifle was too heavy to carry up and down the mountain every day, so I settled for the loan of my father's best hunting knife.

"Why not take along your bow and arrows?" my mother added. "I've seen you practicing and you're a pretty good shot."

"Good thinking, Mom. Besides keeping in practice, I'll have some recreation, too."

On the morning of June 7, 1942, I boarded the train at Sabattis, bound for Nehasane. I was dressed in jeans and a red plaid shirt, and wore my hiking boots. My mother and dad saw me off. As they waved good-bye, they said they hoped all would go well. My bicycle was stowed in the baggage car. The bow and arrows on the seat beside me caused people to look at me suspiciously. When the conductor looked at my ticket and saw that I would be getting off at Nehasane, I thought he looked relieved. My worst embarrassment happened when Shorty, the candy vendor, came through the car and saw my archery set. Only three feet tall, he was a tough little guy, what with years of being teased by the train crew. He stopped beside me and, looking me straight in the eye, said, “Where are you going with those things?”

“I brought them along to practice,” I said defensively.

“You could hurt somebody doing that,” he retorted with a scowl and I heard several people snicker around us.

“Nobody will be near me where I’m going to practice,” I promised him. With that, he went on his way, shaking his head.

When the train whistle signaled for the stop at Nehasane, I gathered up my belongings. The prospect of seeing my friends again excited me. As the train braked to a halt, I caught sight of Mr. Collier standing near his truck. Then, as I alighted, I saw Mrs. Virgil looking my way. I left my baggage there on the ground and hurried to greet them. Mrs. Virgil gave me a big hug and Mr. Collier shook my hand heartily. He then remarked, “You look well, but you’re a little thin.”

“I’ve been away from the mountains too long,” I answered.

We walked over to the station house nearby to greet the Wood family. Pete was sitting in his office chair near the door when I came in. He, too, shook my hand and said, “You’re a sight for sore eyes!” Rose agreed as she clasped both my hands.

“It sure is good to be back,” I said.

In the back of the room, I saw the boy I had noticed standing by the station when I arrived. A shy lad of about twelve, he came forward when Rose asked me if I remembered Luke.

“Of course, but you’ve grown so much.”

“I want to be taller than my dad,” he said, grinning. Pete laughed, and I could see that fair-haired Luke was “the apple of his eye.”

Pete and Rose saw my bicycle and my bow and arrows, and Pete had us all laughing when he said, “If I see a hobo coming up the tracks with an arrow in the seat of his pants, I’ll know where he’s been.”

Riding down to the lodge by the lake, I remarked how familiar things looked. Soon the lodge came into view. As we entered the help's quarters, the first thing I noticed was new paint on the kitchen walls.

"I like that color," I told Mrs. Virgil, who smiled and admitted that she had wanted a "sunny yellow" on the walls. Mr. Collier told me to take a look at the new gas stove.

"We like to keep up with the times," he said. "We got tired of lugging wood, and coal is too dirty, so Mr. Webb gave his O.K."

He showed me how quickly the burners would light, but added, "I shouldn't be showing you this, because you're going to be burning wood in your stove."

"That won't bother me," I answered, "as long as I don't run out."

Mrs. Virgil had a hearty lunch ready and afterwards, when we moved into the living room, I couldn't resist asking Mr. Collier about the fire tower on Mount Electra.

"What will my duties be?"

"You'll need to make out weekly reports for the Conservation Department in Albany. These we will send to Ernest Blue, the district ranger. You will be expected to put in an eight-hour day at the tower, seven days a week if the weather is dry. If it rains and there is no lightning, you may have one or more days off."

"Could I then go home for a short visit?" I asked.

"Yes, but you will have to make sure you carry your Nehasane pass with you. You will need to call Pete Wood in plenty of time so that he can alert the engineer of the stop," Mr. Collier said. He then told me about the two telephones in the tower. "I will explain them better when we get there. You will be able to call the lodge, your cabin, and the observer at the Whitney Park fire tower. Your other duties will include mowing along the trail at the bottom of the mountain for about a hundred yards. As for the trail up the mountain, you should keep an eye open for any trees or large limbs resting on the telephone line. These we will have to remove to keep the line in working order."

"What about my reports to the Conservation Department?"

"Make them out in duplicate each Friday and send them to the regional office in Old Forge. You will also need to check your telephones every day by calling the lodge and the observer on the Whitney fire tower once or twice a week. The telephones should always be ready for use, otherwise you won't be able to report a fire." I nodded, and Mr. Collier got to his feet and said it was time to drive me the four-and-a-half miles to my cabin. Mrs. Virgil rode along with us to see if there was anything I might need at the cabin.

As we drove along in the preserve's Ford truck, I noticed how well maintained the road was. On each hill, I saw an open wooden culvert inserted diagonally into the road. The two-inch opening allowed water to run into it from higher ground, and meant that the road crew could keep it clean easily.

Suddenly, a deer ran across the road ahead of us, then another, followed by twin fawns. When we reached the spot, they had disappeared in the brush. We watched for more, but only saw a mother partridge and her little ones scurry across the road in front of us.

Seeing the deer reminded me of the time when I was in high school and my father loaned me his .25-.20 Winchester rifle. I had a hunting license and occasionally accompanied my father and brother on their hunting jaunts, so I was used to being in the woods.

At the two-mile marker, we caught a glimpse of Nehasane Lake through the trees. It is a long, narrow body of water formed by Beaver River flowing south out of Lake Lila. Here the road turned west. Mrs. Virgil remarked about the abundance of wood ferns growing beside the road. Mr. Collier said it was because the area was shaded by tall trees and was near water.

After many more turns in the road, we came to what was once a vast clearing. The higher ground merged with a swamp and a pond in the distance. Wooded hills surrounded the clearing on all sides, making it a lovely valley.

"What happened here?" I asked, as I realized this was not a natural open space.

"This place was once called Partlow. About forty years ago both Brandreth and Nehasane conducted extensive lumbering operations here and shipped out many flatcars loaded with the finest logs."

Looking around, I noticed an attractive brown cabin set back from the road.

"Is that my new home?" I asked as I surveyed it with a critical eye.

"Yes, that's where you'll be hanging your hat," said Mrs. Virgil.

"Well, it looks good to me, and I'll have lots of light and sunshine."

Mr. Collier parked the truck in the yard, and called my attention to the stream beyond the road. "You can usually tell if it's raining, and how hard, by looking at that stream," he said.

"Let's see inside." My curiosity was mounting and I hoped I would like my new quarters. After Mr. Collier unlocked the door, Mrs. Virgil and I entered. I saw that the white walls were bare. I was disappointed not to see some pictures, but there was a pretty calendar on one wall. Mrs. Virgil and Mr. Collier told me that they had cleaned the cabin, rearranged the furniture, washed the windows, and added pleasant touches like bureau scarves and café curtains. I also noticed that the wood box was filled with dry wood and kindling.

"Thank you both for making this place so livable. I'm sure the observer before me never had it this good."

"We want you to stay. It's important that you do," Mr. Collier said.

Just then, I heard the rumble of a train as it approached the clearing. Headed north, it crossed the center of the valley about a quarter of a mile away. We watched with interest as it disappeared into the forest, and then returned to the business at hand.

"Wow!" I exclaimed, as I sat on the white metal bed, "I've never slept on a double bed. With all this room I won't fall out." Just then, Mr. Collier brought in a box of groceries Mrs. Virgil had put up for me.

"These should last you a few days—until the order you gave me arrives," Mrs. Virgil said. "I called in your order, along with mine, just before we left the lodge."

"Where do they come from?" I asked.

"For years we've patronized a store at Tupper Lake Junction. Sometimes they get the order out the same day," she replied. Then she helped me put away the nonperishable food in the cupboard by the sink. Next to it was the small wood stove that I would use for heat and cooking.

"My mother had a stove like this when I was growing up, so I know how it works," I told her.

Next, Mr. Collier unloaded a large, covered stoneware crock from the truck. He showed me how to arrange it in the brook off to the right of my cabin. Finding a deep place where balsams shaded the water, he immersed the crock nearly to the brim and placed several rocks around it to steady it. In my "cold crock" went a half dozen eggs, a pound of butter, and a quart of milk. Mr. Collier weighed down the lid with a flat rock. Then, as we returned to the cabin, he pointed to a little building in the balsams about fifty feet behind the cabin, "There's your half-moon house, all tidied up for you."

"Oh, thank you," I knew just what he meant. It was my privy in the wild.

Back in the cabin, I noticed for the first time a medium-sized triangular window tucked under the gable at the rear of the building. Covered with a screen, it provided fresh air day and night, but I was to discover that I could do without it on cold mornings. The daylight it let into the cabin seemed wasted on the floor. Mr. Collier helped me move the round table from the corner by the bed to a spot near the center of the room. This was to become my eating, writing, reading, and work table. The light green painted dresser and the clothes closet were on the right, in the corner behind the door. Every object in the room had its place. The bed had squeaky springs—an annoyance at first, but I finally got used to it. The bed was outfitted with a new mattress, which Mrs. Virgil showed me by lifting up the covers. Colorful bedding, a couple of lightweight plaid blankets, and a quilted coverlet that Mrs. Virgil had made completed the look of solid comfort.

"I'm honored to have such a lovely cover on my bed," I said, and gave her a hug of thanks.

Before leaving, Mr. Collier made sure I knew how to use the telephone. "You can call the lodge, the railroad station at Nehasane, and the fire tower. The card above it has all the numbers on it," he said.

"I'll try it out tonight after supper," I replied.

"One more thing. When there's an electrical storm approaching, pull the telephone switch handle down. For safety's sake, this is important. That way, if lightning comes in on the wires, it will follow the water pipe down into the ground." After giving these instructions, he told me to try the switch so I would know exactly what to do.

"O.K., I'll be back in the morning about 8:30 and we'll climb the mountain," he said before departing with Mrs. Virgil.

As I unpacked and put my things away on this pleasant June afternoon, I heard the rumble of a train again. This time it seemed to be louder and more distinct, so I went outside to get a better look. A heavily timbered hill cut off the sound until the southbound train came into view. I realized that if I listened carefully, I could tell which direction a train was traveling. There would be many rumbles I found out, both day and night, as passenger and freight trains made their daily runs between Utica and Montreal.

— Three —

Off to Find the Tower

On my second day in camp, after a breakfast of cold cereal and scrambled eggs, I heard Mr. Collier's truck stop at the edge of the yard. I looked at my watch. It was 8:30. My lunch was already in my knapsack, so I picked up my jacket and hurried out the door. I had been out earlier looking for the tower, but had not seen it. When Mr. Collier opened the truck door, I greeted him and asked, "Where in the world is the tower? I haven't been able to spot it."

"It's off to the south behind Partlow Hill, over there." He pointed to the thickly wooded rise around which the northbound train had appeared. "You may catch a glimpse of it just beyond the railroad tracks."

Then we were off. We skirted the wide stream in the clearing, then crossed the tracks a quarter mile beyond. I looked back at the cabin and was pleased to see how well it blended into the morning shadows. We continued west through a beautiful section of the valley. Within a few feet of the road, we passed a couple of lovely ponds surrounded by swamp grasses and small balsams and tamaracks, whose profiles were reflected on their mirror-like surfaces. Black ducks and mallards took wing as we approached. I was so engrossed that I forgot to look for the tower until we had passed the vantage point. Mr. Collier laughed at my consternation and said, "You'll have plenty of chances to look for it when you start riding your bike to the trail."

"How far does this road go?" I asked.

"About six miles farther. It ends at Gull Lake. I'll be putting out rock salt for the deer in a week or ten days. You can ride along if you don't have to be at the tower."

"Yes, I'd like to," I replied. "It would help me learn the lay of the land."

The distance from my cabin to the beginning of the trail up Mount Electra was only three-quarters of a mile. This I knew from having studied a map of the park back at the lodge. As we drove, Mr. Collier filled me in on the morning updates he had heard over radio station WGY in Schenectady. He thought that the news about the war in Europe was not encouraging. Then he changed the subject to explain how important it was that I remember to check the telephone lines along the trail.

"We'll make a couple calls on the phones at the tower, just to be sure they are working right."

I had anticipated this day for the past two months. Now it was finally here. I found myself excitedly enjoying each new incident. As the truck slowed down, I saw a sign on a tree beside the road. All it said was "Trail."

"Is this where the trail starts?" I asked as I noticed a cleared place on the left side of the road.

"Yes," he said, "See those balsams over there? Behind them would be a good place to conceal your bike."

"How far is the hike up the mountain?" I asked, as we got out of the truck.

"It's less than a mile and it's not a hard climb. You will learn to pace yourself," Mr. Collier said.

A small log bridge marked the beginning of the trail. The ground appeared level as I looked ahead through the marsh grass. I could see that the path wound along the base of the mountain for several hundred feet, skirting a big swamp.

As we walked along, I noticed that tall grasses leaned over the trail. Soon Mr. Collier stopped and pointed to a nearby maple tree from which hung a farmer's scythe.

"Do you know what that is?" he asked.

"Sure," I replied, "It's a scythe for cutting grass or hay."

"Have you ever used one?"

"No, but I've watched my father use one."

Mr. Collier lifted it from the crotch in the tree, took a sharpening stone out of his pocket, and showed me how to sharpen the long, curved blade. Making several strikes of the stone along the cutting edge, he carefully let it slide off the blade each time. After testing the sharpness with his finger, he proceeded to trim the grass on each side of the trail. Cutting the grass stirred up a cloud of black flies. I reached into my knapsack for a bottle of citronella, and quickly dabbed the pungent dope on my face, neck, and clothing. Mr. Collier did the same. This stopped the flies from biting, but they still annoyed us. Then it was my turn to try out the scythe. After grasping the two handles, I found that I could swing it easily. To my surprise, I handled it well, and soon was cutting the grass. Mr. Collier looked on approvingly. As I swung the blade into a thick clump of marsh grass, I suddenly felt it clank into a rock with a horrible scraping sound. I recoiled with a cry of dismay.

"I forgot to tell you to beware of hidden rocks," Mr. Collier said with a grin. "Let's see the end of the blade." Sure enough, it was bent where it had hit the rock.

"Sorry about that," I murmured. "Can it be straightened?"

"Oh yes, but you can still mow with it." With that, he took the scythe, carefully wiped the blade dry with a rag, and hung it in another crotched tree.

We walked on. Near the base of the mountain, where the trail began the ascent, Mr. Collier reached into his pocket and pulled out a bread wrapper containing a couple of slices of stale bread. Rustling the paper sack, he called out, "Here Nanny, come and get it." Soon a handsome doe came bounding toward us through brush and balsams, but the sight of two people caused her to slow up as she approached. Cautiously she walked up to Mr. Collier when she saw the bread he was holding out. I thought how pretty she was in her sleek, red summer coat. Her delicate ears twitched as she discouraged the flies that had followed her. I couldn't help but think of Bambi when I looked at her soft eyes.

"When Broughton was the fire observer last summer, Nanny was his pet," Mr. Collier explained.

"Does she stay around here all the time?"

"Yes, this is her home territory, so you will see her often if you have something for her to eat." Nanny took the bread eagerly and we watched her for a couple minutes. Then we started up the trail, but she just stood there contentedly finishing the bread.

I was glad to see that we were climbing the north slope where it was cooler. My thoughts turned to Mount Electra, the name given it by the Webb family. It was named, I had learned, for Electra Havermeyer, the wife of J. Watson Webb, the present owner. I preferred this name from Greek mythology to the less colorful name of Rock Lake Mountain, as it was known in the Conservation Department records. There were three steep sections of the trail. Near the base of the second one, we came upon a spring of running water. Here Mr. Collier filled his flask, saying we would surely need a drink when we reached the top.

"Fill your water jug here. No better water anywhere."

"I'm glad it's near the trail," I replied.

As we climbed, we heard the songs of several birds. One in particular caught our attention. It had a lovely, flute-likc quality and was so beautiful that we stood to listen.

"What bird is that?" I asked.

"I believe it's a thrush, but there are several different kinds. Sure is a pretty song."

After climbing a couple of hundred feet, we stopped again to rest. This gave me an opportunity to ask Mr. Collier another question.

"Did Mr. Broughton have many visitors at the tower?"

"He had a few, only two or three.

"Oh, I hope I have more than that," I exclaimed, rather disappointed. "I'd like to show people the view and point out interesting places."

"I think you'll have some visitors when the word gets out that you're up here. Remember, though, this is a private preserve, so no trespassing is allowed." With that, we continued up the trail. Upon reaching the summit, we were refreshed by a cool breeze out of the west—nature's own solace sighing in the spruces around us. I looked around expectantly.

"Where is the tower?"

"Up ahead. We're almost there."

The trail followed the ridge at the top of the mountain and continued out of sight under the spruce trees. Overhead branches prevented me from seeing the tower until we were nearly upon it. Then I saw the steel girders of the base of the tower firmly anchored into a rock foundation.

I gazed upward, and the height of the fire tower caused me to catch my breath. I counted nine flights of stairs. "About seventy feet," Mr. Collier said, anticipating my question.

"Wow! Talk about a tall tower."

"It had to be high to get the tower room well above the trees. It is one of the highest in the Adirondacks."

As I stood looking up at it, I wondered if I would trip and fall or lose my balance on those open stairs. The skimpy railings didn't seem to offer much protection either.

A drink of water from the flask refreshed me and I saw Mr. Collier give me a challenging look. I made up my mind that I wasn't going to be intimidated.

"I'm ready," I said in as steady a voice as I could. Up one flight of stairs and then another, we slowly climbed. About forty feet up, the wind felt stronger, and I glanced down at the ground.

"Oh-h-h," I said. "I had better not look down."

"You might as well get used to it now," Mr. Collier said. "That way, it won't bother you later."

I forced myself to look down again and grasped the railing as if my life depended on it. After climbing to the eighth landing, I had to take a rest. We were now above the trees. Gazing about, I saw a whole new world spread out before me. Mountain ranges, blue in the distance, and lakes and ponds were scattered everywhere.

When we reached the top, Mr. Collier pushed open the trap door and we entered the tower room. Stepping aside, he dropped the door back in place, where it became part of the floor. The opening measured about two feet by four feet, just large enough to allow a person to pass through. And I noticed a large steel hook on the side of the wall to hold the door open. I turned back to the view.

The canopy of green treetops looked like a softly patterned rug spread out below me. Lakes and ponds shone silvery as they reflected the overcast sky. I was delighted. How exhilarating! I could tell that Mr. Collier also appreciated the view, although he didn't say much. Then I realized he had seen it all many times before.

I looked around the room, which appeared to be about seven feet square. Bolted to the center of the floor stood a round, high table with a map under heavy glass. The steel side panels of the walls were about six feet high and included large windows, two on each side. Every other one could be opened. This would be important, Mr. Collier pointed out, when an observer had to study smoke through binoculars and needed the clearest view. Reaching into his knapsack, he pulled out a pair of binoculars in a black case and handed them to me.

"These are 8 x 40 power and of very good quality. Keep them here in their waterproof case."

The map under the glass was a U.S. Geological Survey topographical map that showed the surrounding countryside to a point fifteen miles in all directions. Fastened to the center of the table was a pivoting metal pointer, or alidade. Distances in miles were marked along its length. Mr. Collier explained how a person could line up actual places on the terrain below by using the alidade. With the circular map and the pointer, he identified the prominent mountains for me: Blue Mountain to the east, Kempshall Mountain to the northeast near the foot of Long Lake, and Mount Morris far to the north near Tupper Lake. Farther to my left was Mount Arab, west of Tupper Lake. He also pointed out Cat Mountain south of Cranberry Lake and West Mountain west of Raquette Lake.

We counted fifteen bodies of water, among them nearby Rock Lake with its irregular shoreline. By lining it up with the alidade, I discovered this lake was about one mile south of the tower. I asked Mr. Collier why I couldn't find Owls Head Mountain near the upper end of Long Lake.

"Let's take a look," he suggested. Comparing the view eastward with the map, Mr. Collier concluded that Albany Mountain partly obscured Salmon Lake Mountain, which in turn hid Owls Head from view.

"Oh," I said somewhat disappointed, "I'll have to be content with Kempshall as my home landmark."

From his knapsack, Mr. Collier then pulled out a bundle of papers.

"These are the Conservation Department forms for your weekly reports. Follow the instructions and send them to District Ranger Ernest Blue at Old Forge each weekend."

"If you don't happen to come by the cabin, I will have a good excuse to ride up to the lodge with my report; then I can say hello to everybody."

Mr. Collier next explained how to use the two telephones.

"This is the metallic line," he said, pointing to the smaller one. "It connects Nehasane, Brandreth, and Whitney Parks. The other phone is for Nehasane only. It connects the lodge on Lake Lila and the other Webb camps to the railroad station, the tower, and your cabin. Part of your job will be to check the telephone lines that follow the trail up to the tower. Call in each morning by ringing the superintendent's number. It will ring where Mrs. Virgil or I can hear it. When you first reach the tower, flip this switch up to connect the telephone service. Don't forget to disconnect it when you leave for the day."

"What if I can't get through to the lodge?" I asked.

"Keep trying for half an hour, then if there's no answer, try Pete Wood at the station. If you still can't reach anyone, go down the trail, checking the line carefully as you go. Continue on to your cabin and try calling from there. If there's no answer, ride to the lodge, again checking the telephone line along the way. If we can't reach you either at the tower or your cabin after a reasonable time, we'll investigate."

"Does wind or lightning account for most problems with the telephones?" I asked.

"Wind causes the most problems, and knocks over trees that take the lines down. If you're on the trail and it's a windy day, watch for limbs that could come down on you. Let's try out the line now so you can hear what a good connection sounds like."

Using the crank on the side of the phone, he rang the number at the lodge. Mrs. Virgil answered and reported good reception. She asked what the weather and the view were like. Mr. Collier handed the phone to me so I could talk to her. She told me she'd like to climb Mount Electra some day. I assumed she was kidding, so I replied, "Sure, why not?" and we both laughed.

When I hung up, Mr. Collier asked me to disengage the telephone switch. We then closed and bolted the windows in preparation for leaving the tower. He pulled up the trap door, and held it while I started down the steps. As he followed, he showed me how to lower the door.

As I descended I held onto the railing tightly and concentrated on the steps. The stiff west wind rattled a part of the steel tower. When a gust hit me, my hat blew off. I watched with dismay as it went swirling down, nearly lodging in a tree.

"Your hat's in more of a hurry to get down than you are!" quipped Mr. Collier.

"Well, I've got more sense than it has," I retorted, and kept a firm grip on the railing. Halfway down I took one look at the ground and said to myself, "Will I ever get used to this awful height?"

After descending the mountain, Mr. Collier dropped me off at my new home. I had had an exciting time and learned a lot. That evening, the events of the day kept running through my mind. As the sun sank behind the hills beyond the clearing, I turned in for my first night alone in the wilderness.

— Four —

An Exciting New Life

It has been said that the cowboy's best friend is his horse, but mine was my bicycle. To protect it from the heavy dew I covered it at night with my poncho and parked it under the eaves against the cabin wall. Nearly every morning I rode it to the beginning of the mountain trail and back in the afternoon. Two or three times a week I pedaled over to the lodge for my mail, or to post my reports to the Conservation Department.

One evening in early June, as I walked around my yard in the clearing, a plan for a flowerbed came to me. I decided to plant a double row of nasturtiums on each side of the path to my door. They were easy to grow and they would provide lots of color.

My cabin had only cold running water. This meant I'd have to heat water on the wood stove for washing dishes and bathing. There was no electricity, and I missed the convenience of a refrigerator, or even an icebox. Before nearly every meal, I had to make a trip out to the crock in the brook. I had no radio for news or music, so from time to time I would phone Mrs. Virgil to find out about any important events. She asked if I would like a couple of magazines to read, and said she'd send them along with my mail. With no electric lights, I was often in bed by 9:30. My days were so full that I found myself retiring earlier than I was used to.

I renamed Partlow, where my cabin was located, Green Valley because the grasses in the clearing were a bright green, a color that contrasted with the surrounding dark forest. With a few exceptions, every species of wild animal native to the Adirondacks made their home in the woods around me. I was told that panthers, wolves, and moose no longer inhabited the area; that they had been killed off before the end of the last century. But there were black bears, and I knew that, sooner or later, I would meet up with one.

After a few days, I overcame the "terror of the tower" and was no longer scared to look down as I climbed the stairs. Hiking up the mountain also became easier as my muscles adjusted to the exercise. From the start, I enjoyed my fire observer duties because I liked being outdoors, and I found myself wishing there might be a future in it. Climbing a mountain in summer was often warm work. I found that out when I carried my lunch, a light jacket in case of cold wind or rain, and a gallon jug half full of water. Every other morning, I would stop at the spring and half fill the jug with fresh water. At the tower, I first checked the telephone lines by calling the lodge twice a day and the neighboring parks twice a week. The first time I called the fire observer on Salmon Lake Mountain in Whitney Park, a gruff voice answered after I had rung the number three times.

"Hello, hello, who's calling?" My female voice must have startled him, for when I told him my name and asked for his, the reply, "Bill Touhey," was subdued. I told him I was the new observer on Mount Electra. He was silent for a moment and then said, "Well, I'll be!" But he soon warmed up and it wasn't long before we were comparing notes about which towers and what bodies of water we could see. He also told me that Bill Black, a man I knew from Long Lake, was the State forest ranger stationed at Sabattis.

Later, I asked Mr. Collier if he knew Bill Touhey.

"Bill has been the observer on Salmon Lake Mountain for quite a few years. So you made his acquaintance?"

"Yes, he was a bit gruff at first, but I'm sure we both enjoyed the visit. He knows every mountain and lake for miles around."

"That's good," Mr. Collier said. "If you spot any suspicious smoke, check with Bill."

"How old is he?"

"He's an older gent. When he was young, he had red hair and a temper to match it."

"That's interesting," I said, "But I'll bet he likes his job, and likes to be alone."

The problem of getting food to my cabin was not as difficult as I had imagined. All my groceries were shipped in on the railroad from the store near Tupper Lake—usually three or four days after I had placed my order. When they arrived at the lodge, Mrs. Virgil stored the perishables in the icebox until Mr. Collier brought them to me, often the same day. I kept my cupboard well stocked with canned fruits and vegetables and some Dinty Moore stew. Each delivery included fresh meat, and I always used it up first. I was not good at wilderness cooking and I didn't have many utensils to work with. I didn't have much inspiration, either, with no one but myself to cook for. Cooking on my stove, I ruefully thought, was like cooking on a camping trip. At least it was, however, on a bit of a grander scale and the food didn't taste smoky.

A soaker of a storm hit in the middle of June, one that started with an all-night rain. It was still raining the next morning when I awoke. Knowing I could take the day off, I breathed a sigh of contentment, rolled over, and went back to sleep. That day was a relaxed one. I completed my chores and wrote some letters, including one to Howard. I realized I had not heard from him in quite awhile. I wondered about him and hoped he was all right.

That evening, I noticed that the nearby stream had risen. It was still raining, and I was thankful that the roof didn't leak. Suddenly, I remembered my perishables out in the crock. Had they been inundated or washed away? I flew out the door and ran to the spring. I found the crock leaning downstream with water seeping into it. I yanked the whole business out of the torrent and drained it, remembering to grab the milk bottle and set it on the ground. The rain let up for a short time, so I went looking for three stones large enough to place under the crock to raise it well above the waterline. The ones I found did the trick and I resettled the perishables and hoped for the best.

Monday morning brought more surprises. The rain had finally stopped, but it was a mighty wet day. As I rode to the beginning of the trail, I noticed that the big stream beyond the railroad tracks had risen at least a foot. Yet I didn't think to be alarmed. As I pedaled, I marveled at the changes in the scenery.

When I arrived at the trail, however, I became apprehensive. The bridge and even the road were under water and the trail was submerged under six inches of water for more than fifty feet. Only in a few places were the old corduroy logs visible. I soon realized my predicament, but couldn't think about turning back. My job required crossing the flooded trail and climbing the mountain. I found a new place back along the road to conceal my bike, then I went looking for something to ford the trail. I found a couple of old boards and a frail ladder and I managed to get across on these.

At the foot of the trail, I found a rock to sit on, took off the wet boots, and wrung out my socks. As I was doing this, I spied Nanny not far away watching me and, no doubt, wondering what this was all about. Having wet feet and boots for my efforts didn't put me in the best of moods, so all Nanny got was a grouchy "Hello there." I trudged along the trail in my wet boots but changed to dry shoes once I reached the tower room. When I checked in, Mr. Collier answered the phone. After telling him about crossing the flooded trail, I got the nearest thing to a scolding I had had in a long time.

"You don't need to be at the tower after an all-day rain," he said sharply. "Let that be a lesson for you to take better care of yourself!"

"Yes sir," I answered lamely before he hung up. I brooded for the rest of the morning. Then the sky cleared, the sun shone, and the wet world around me began to dry out. I decided to leave the tower and get in some archery practice. A few days earlier, I had brought along the potato sack that Mr. Collier had given me for a target. Stuffed full of leaves, the open end tied with string, the sack would have to do until I made some paper targets to pin on it. I propped it up against a bush higher up the slope in the little clearing below the tower. Because the target was level with my head, it wasn't the best location.

After I had taken four or five shots at the sack, missing some of them, I heard a twig snap in the woods nearby. Alert, I stood still

Sabattis Station, May 1952. *Courtesy Adirondack Museum*

Nehasane Station, 1925. *Courtesy Adirondack Museum*

George Collier, Superintendent of Nehasane Park, 1938–1950.
Courtesy Adirondack Museum

Mrs. Virgil with one of the Webb family's Shelburne terriers.

Forest Lodge on Lake Lila, the summer camp of the Webb family. Photograph by T.E. Marr, 1890s. *Courtesy Adirondack Museum*

Forest Lodge and boat house (building at left) on Lake Lila. Most of the lodge was used by the Webb family with the spectacular game room at the left. The kitchen and dining room were in the center, the help's quarters on the right. Photograph by T.E. Marr, 1890s. *Courtesy Adirondack Museum*

Forest Lodge on Lake Lila with Mount Frederica in the background. It looked much the same in the 1940s. Photograph by T.E. Marr, 1890s.

Courtesy Adirondack Museum

Living room at Forest Lodge, also known as the game room, with its spectacular fireplace. Note the mounted panther standing on the ledge above the fireplace. Photograph by T.E. Marr, 1890s.
Courtesy Adirondack Museum

The main dining room at Forest Lodge. Photograph by T.E. Marr, 1890s.
Courtesy Adirondack Museum

William Seward Webb sitting just outside his bedroom on the porch of Forest Lodge. He built the first railroad through the Adirondacks in the 1890s. Photograph by T.E. Marr, 1890s. *Courtesy Adirondack Museum*

J. Watson Webb, son of William Seward Webb, was the owner of Nehasane Park when the author worked there in 1942. *Courtesy Adirondack Museum.*

Howard Seaman takes a break from road work at Nehasane Park.

Tuffy, left, and Howard, right, toast sandwiches for lunch.

and waited. A small balsam tree quivered as something brushed against it. Then I caught a glimpse of a dark animal the size of a large dog moving quickly through the underbrush. It disappeared before I could get a good look at it. Probably it was a yearling bear that must have "winded" me, because it sure left in a hurry.

Having lost interest in my target practice, I gathered up my arrows and headed up to the tower room where I ate my lunch as I studied the landscape around me. To the northeast, a couple of hawks circled high above the swamp. I watched as one of them suddenly dove straight down and disappeared from view behind tall spruces. Farther to the left, I could see Green Valley lying peacefully in the bright sunshine. A movement there caught my eye; it was the north-bound train.

The noon hour was so quiet that I became bored. I picked up one of my magazines to look through for the third time. Finding nothing of interest, I tossed it into my knapsack to take home and discard. Realizing that I did not need to be on duty, I decided to start work on my flowerbeds at the cabin. Before leaving, I had a look around one last time to be sure no smoke was visible, disconnected the telephone, closed the trap door, and left. Upon reaching the lower end of the trail, I realized that I had to cross the flooded swamp again. Annoyed at finding the water even deeper, I just waded across. Back at the cabin, I took off my wet boots and stuffed them full of crumpled newspaper. That evening I had a fire in the stove to warm the place up and my boots dried overnight.

The next day I returned to my flowerbed project as soon as I arrived back from the tower. I knew where tools were stored under the back of the cabin. Picking out a shovel and rake, I found the digging difficult. The thick quack grass almost defeated me. Finally, I succeeded in making a border of dirt a foot wide on each side of the path. Unfortunately, I had forgotten to order the flower seeds and it was a week before they came. When they arrived, I planted all of them that same evening.

My job on the mountain was a nine-to-five proposition, hours that suited me. On some days, the weather influenced my moods.

If it was dark and cloudy, I occasionally felt depressed and lonely, but knew the best antidote was to keep busy. I wanted to hear the news and listen to some music, but I didn't have a radio. The next time I could get some time off to go home, I planned to return with a good battery-powered radio.

When I called in to sign off from the tower one afternoon, Mrs. Virgil caused a bit of excitement in my solitary world. She told me that the Webb family had arrived on the noon train. She hadn't seen Mr. Collier for hours because he was busy getting them settled in. I could picture all the bustle and wondered if there were any young people in the group. A couple of days later, I asked Mr. Collier about it and he said, "Most of the family is here, and they're a lively bunch. They've kept me running seeing to it that everything's in working order."

"Are there any young people among them?"

"Yes, but they won't bother you," he replied, "though Mr. Webb may stop by to say hello, because I told him about you."

A few days later, I did in fact meet Mr. Webb. I had just parked my bike against the cabin when I heard a car approaching, one I had noticed following me at a distance across the valley. Mr. Webb, who had a guest with him, hailed me, "How do you like it up on the mountain? Aren't you afraid of the bears?"

"Not at all. I haven't even seen one yet." I replied. "And, as for the tower job, I love it."

Mr. Webb smiled and then introduced his guest, whose name I did not catch. It sounded foreign, but I was at a loss to remember it.

"You look like the job agrees with you," Mr. Webb remarked and his guest nodded in agreement.

"I eat and sleep well, I assure you." I thought both men looked like English aristocrats in their stylish tweeds and sporty felt hats.

"We must be on our way," Mr. Webb concluded, as he touched his finger to his hat and shifted his Ford touring car into gear. Soon they disappeared down the road and into the woods. Was I imagining it or did Mr. Webb seem a bit stiff and not as friendly as I remembered? Perhaps it was because of his companion, I thought.

Before another week was up, the weather turned rainy again and I was able to take a few days off. I took the train to Sabattis where my dad met me at the busy station. On the road to Long Lake he filled me in on the news, both local and national, and how the war was going. Coming out of Nehasane's solitude, I realized how much I had been missing. It seemed like life and the world were passing me by.

I told my dad how I missed not having a radio and he agreed to loan me one. Being home, even for a couple days, rejuvenated my spirits. I was comforted seeing my parents and brother, answering their questions, and telling them about my life in the woods. I was also curious about my younger sisters, both of whom were working in Syracuse at the time.

Riding the train back to Nehasane, thoughts of those at home and in the service kept running through my mind and I worried that some of my loved ones would be drawn into the fighting. But these thoughts quickly disappeared when I heard the whistle blow for my stop.

The radio that I borrowed changed my life at my cabin and the tower. It made the days more meaningful and pleasant and the evenings less lonely. Every morning I listened to the news from WGY, and some evenings tuned in to country music programs.

My bicycle allowed me to explore the area beyond where the trail to the tower started. Mrs. Virgil told me about the lovely ponds—she mentioned Wilder, Niger, and Partlow—farther along the road, and I checked them out on the U.S.G.S. topographical map in the tower. I had also heard about a camp on the shore of Gull Lake, where the road ended. I felt I simply had to see these places.

My chance came one afternoon as the sky cleared after a good rain, and, freed from my tower duties, I started out with a light heart. The well-maintained dirt road lured me on, up and down the hills under a shady canopy of trees. Occasionally, a real hill brought my feet to the ground and I would walk my bike to the top. As I pedaled, chipmunks and red squirrels announced my invasion of their territory. When I rounded one turn, a partridge departed in haste after I surprised it strutting across the road. A little farther on, I noticed that balsams began to replace the hardwoods in the forest around me and I found myself riding on lower ground.

As I approached a pond, I suddenly heard voices and saw water shining through the trees. Some people must be camping or fishing, I thought. Immediately I stopped, realizing I wasn't supposed to be there. I was only an employee, and it wouldn't do to have any of the Webbs know, even if the woods were still wet, that I wasn't manning the fire tower. Reluctantly I returned to Green Valley, disappointed and unhappy with the abrupt end of my adventure.

As I approached my cabin, Mr. Collier drove up and stopped his familiar green truck in front of the cabin. I pedaled faster and called out a greeting as he alighted. He had mail and groceries for me, a diversion that turned my day around. Mr. Collier, however, didn't know why I was so pleased to see him and I thought it best not to mention my excursion.

One evening early in July, I sat in my cabin listening to country music on the radio. The weather had been cloudy all afternoon and darkness descended over Green Valley earlier than usual. For that reason, I called it a day and retired, but sleep eluded me. It must have been ten o'clock or later when I was startled by the sound of a car approaching the cabin. I heard voices, one deeper than the rest though they all sounded to be about my age. Someone called my name, entreating me to get up and open the door.

"We're from the lodge and would like to get acquainted."

I jumped out of bed and somehow got decently dressed, but became more indignant by the minute. I could hear someone playing a mouth organ and a voice now and then. I sputtered to myself that those people ought to know better than to come calling at this hour. I grabbed my flashlight and picked up the poker by the stove. Unlocking the door and opening it halfway, I shone the light in their faces and raised the poker above my head.

"You fellows have some nerve coming here and expecting me to let you in. I don't even know you. Now get away from here!"

"We only wanted to get acquainted," one of them said defensively.

"If you want to get acquainted, come back in the daytime," I answered more amicably.

Their faces showed surprise and dismay. I don't think that they had ever been confronted like this before. They retreated to their car, and I watched to be sure that they drove away. As soon as they were gone, remorse got the best of me. Perhaps I was too hard on them. After all, they didn't threaten me. What must they think? Needless to say, they never returned. I worried that Mr. Webb would find out about this escapade and question or scold me, but he never did.

During my stay at Nehasane, I kept track of all my expenses. I was surprised how much I had paid for postage stamps at the end of the first month. I had spent $1.70, and had written many letters, but with stamps costing three cents to post a letter, it was a bargain. Since I could only telephone the lodge and the neighboring preserves, my family and friends had to hear from me via the post office at Nehasane Station. I dropped off my mail at the lodge, and Mr. Collier would pick it up on his daily trip to the station.

My dad was a devoted letter writer, as was my mother. I had younger brothers and sisters, and several relatives with whom I kept in contact. Last but not least, I wrote to Howard at Langley Field in Virginia. It was less of a duty than a pleasure to stay in touch with him and keep him informed of news on the home front.

Mrs. Virgil performed a real service by sorting my mail. Over the phone, she would read the postmarks and names on letters waiting for me at the lodge. If I wanted them that evening, and there was no chance of their being brought to me, I'd bicycle to the lodge to pick them up. Once in awhile, Mrs. Virgil would invite me to stay for supper, and that was a special treat.

"So you get tired of your own cooking, eh?" she would tease. One time she prepared a large dish of cottage cheese. When I told her how good it tasted, she said it was time that I learned how to make it. She wrote the recipe down for me, specifying sour milk, of which I had some nearly every week. Using whole milk, my first batch turned out great, and I enjoyed making it often.

When I planned my own supper, I made the bike trip later for my mail. One evening late in July, I started about 6:30 and had not proceeded a mile when adventure caught up with me. As I rounded a turn in the road, I heard a strange, deep noise. Then I heard it again and realized I had startled a bear and it was growling at me. I didn't look around as I pedaled away from there with all the speed I could muster.

When I reached the lodge, everyone looked at me in surprise when I called out, "I've been initiated at last!"

"I'll bet you finally saw a bear?" Mrs. Virgil guessed.

"No, not quite, but one growled at me when I surprised it near the road," and I told them about my encounter.

"I think you really want to see a bear," Mr. Collier teased. "We'll see if it can be arranged."

The sun was getting ready to set when I suddenly realized I had the return ride ahead of me. There was no time to lose. I gathered up my mail, fastened the strap on the mail pouch, and hurried outside to my bike. Mrs. Virgil followed me out and said, "Don't forget what I told you about making noise. Give a yell now and then to scare away any bears."

"O.K., I will," I said as I swung onto the bike seat.

The road was level for the first mile and I made good time. A couple of deer ran along the road ahead of me until I practiced my yell. That sent them into the woods. By the time I reached the three-mile marker beyond Nehasane Lake, it was getting dark. I rounded a turn, and saw a dark object on the side of the road. I yelled, but whatever it was did not move. As I came nearer, I recognized with relief that I had shouted at a stump. Half a mile farther, another black form appeared. No amount of yelling scared it, and this one turned out to be a big boulder. Perspiration ran down my face, and my clothes felt clammy. All the while, the road and the woods were getting darker, and I yelled more often. Finally, I came out into my clearing, where it was a little less dark.

There was my cabin. It had never looked so good.

— Five —

All of My Neighbors Are Wild

Nehasane Park had a sizable deer population. It was not unusual to see several does in one day along its roads. At this time of year, I often saw them with their fawns looking handsome in their reddish-tan coats. They could be seen best near the salt licks along the road. These "licks" were large hardwood stumps, old but not decayed. In crevices on top, Mr. Collier would place large chunks of rock salt. Since deer crave salt in their diet during hot weather, it wasn't long before they discovered these stumps. They would lick the salt and salty wood creating deep grooves in the stumps. Each June Mr. Collier made a special trip dispensing salt chunks along the ten-mile road from the lodge to Gull Lake. One Saturday morning, after a heavy shower in the night, Mr. Collier drove out to check on the condition of the road to Gull Lake. As he came by the cabin, he saw me working in my flowerbed and stopped his truck.

"I'll be putting out salt chunks for the deer tomorrow afternoon. Do you want to ride up to Gull Lake?"

"Sure, count me in."

"All right, I'll be along about 1:30," he said, and was on his way.

The next day, he brought Mrs. Virgil along with him. On our outing, we saw all kinds of deer: small ones, large ones, some with small antlers, even a part albino one. Most of them bounded away as the truck approached.

"I wish they would stand still longer," Mrs. Virgil complained.

"Can't expect them to be as tame as those in our backyard," Mr. Collier replied.

As the truck rounded one curve, we surprised twin fawns standing in the middle of the road. Their mother had just crossed it, and stood watching a few feet away. As we approached, the fawns became frightened and confused. One ran to the right, the other to the left. Mr. Collier slammed on the brakes. One fawn darted back across the road in front of us, and joined his twin and distraught mother. They then disappeared into the woods.

"Wow!" I exclaimed. "That was exciting."

"I'll bet mother deer is giving her kids a piece of her mind," Mrs. Virgil said.

As we drove along, my anticipation grew. At last, I would get to see a part of the preserve that I had heard so much about.

Now and then Mr. Collier would stop the truck, reach for a chunk of salt, and wade through the brush to a stump at the edge of the woods, where he would tap a salt chunk securely into the recess of the stump so that the deer would not be able to dislodge it.

After a while, I noticed that the road was leading to lower ground.

"Here's Partlow Lake. It's a wild and beautiful place," Mr. Collier said. "One of Mr. Webb's sons wants to build a camp here someday."

What a gem it was. Near the road we saw a small, balsam-lined bay and, looking out over the water, we had a delightful view of the opposite shore. Then a couple miles farther, we arrived at Niger Lake. Narrower and longer than Partlow Lake, it was surrounded by steep forested hills. Our last stop was Gull Lake at the end of the road. Here and there, we saw large boulders that showed above its waters and made good resting and nesting places for gulls. The big rustic cabin near the shore looked impressive and reminded me of a hunting camp.

Before we reached the end of the road, we saw so many deer we lost count and Mr. Collier continued dispensing the rock salt until it was all gone. On our return, we noticed that several deer had already found the chunks of salt. At one stump, a porcupine was busy getting in a few licks.

There was an old hardwood stump some two hundred feet from my cabin, one that had been used as a salt lick for many years. When people were at the cabin, the deer stayed away, but evenings when I was alone, they would approach the stump. The more deer that came, the more interesting they were to watch. Deer behavior, I thought, often resembles human behavior. Some in the group were bossy while others always got picked on or were chased away without getting a taste of the salt. One large doe was especially selfish and crowded all others aside. Another one acted like a tyrant, not budging when challenged. At times she would stand on her hind legs and lash out with her sharp hooves at her opponents. Occasionally, as many as a dozen deer would appear. They kept their feelings to themselves, for I seldom heard any one of them make a sound as I watched them through the window. Yet they did communicate. I used to see them strike the ground with a front hoof, especially when they became alarmed.

I saw the first muskrat I had ever seen in the wild at Green Valley. A small creature with a rat-like tail and water-soaked fur, it came out of a nearby pond, climbed up on a rock, and proceeded to eat a root delicacy it had found. Another time, as I bicycled to the lodge, I saw a fisher at the place where the road led up a slight grade near the two-mile marker. I was pedaling slowly. Suddenly I heard a commotion at the edge of the woods. An animal that I thought resembled a cross between a fox and a black cat was looking at me curiously. Not until I spoke did it disappear. I was sure it was a fisher and Mr. Collier agreed when I described it to him.

One of my duties was keeping the mountain trail mowed where the swamp grasses grew. If I thought I had finished the job when I had cleared that section once with the scythe, I was mistaken. A couple of mornings each week I brought along the sharpening stone, lifted the scythe from the crotch of the tree and sharpened it. Then I proceeded mowing where I had left off, cutting a neat four-foot-wide swath. When I had enough, I hung the scythe up in the fork of another tree. All summer long I cleared the trail, though few actually saw my work.

Each time I climbed the mountain, I looked forward to seeing Nanny, the tame deer, at the foot of the trail. Knowing when I would be along, she was usually close by. I saved stale crusts of bread and occasionally an apple for her. All I had to do was call her name and rustle the bread paper and she'd come on the run. If I was a bit slow in getting bread out of the bag, she'd start nosing after it impatiently. Several other deer lived in the area but they were wary of humans. Once in awhile, I would see one or more standing at a distance watching me as I fed Nanny and less often I would spot a handsome eight-point buck with antlers "in the velvet."

As the weeks went by, I still had not seen a bear, and was beginning to feel indifferent about meeting one. On one occasion at the tower, I missed seeing what I thought was a bear, for I heard shambling about in the underbrush below me. I buckled on my hunting knife to bolster my courage and went down the steps to investigate. I heard noises in the woods below my archery range, but they became less audible each time I paused to listen. Whatever it was, it must have picked up my scent and slipped away. Mr. Collier had told me earlier that last summer my predecessor at the tower had seen a bear several times, so I was disappointed.

As the weather got warmer, my daily climb up the mountain made me decide that I needed to get my shoulder-length hair cut shorter. When I asked Mrs. Virgil, she told me she knew of a beauty salon in Saranac Lake that I could walk to from the train station. I made an appointment, stayed overnight at the lodge, and next morning rode to the station with Mr. Collier. He told me to flag the train myself. As it approached, we could hear it a quarter of a mile down the tracks. Then it came into view, rounding the curve at a good speed. I was a bit scared, but I stood near the tracks waving the flag, and faced that big locomotive bearing down on me. The train was almost beside me when the engineer decided to stop. The brakes screeched and the conductors appeared to find out what had happened. Passengers pressed against the windows, peering out. I had a long trot to reach the first car, where a conductor hailed me, "Are you the only passenger?"

"I am," I answered breathlessly, adding, "Good heavens! I thought the train wasn't going to stop." The conductor made sure I was safely aboard, then signaled the engineer to proceed. After he punched my round-trip ticket, I settled down to enjoy the ride. Awhile later, Shorty came up the aisle, carrying his basket of candy bars. I was in too good a mood to argue with him, besides I wanted something to supplement my lunch. Holding out my money, I said I'd like a Hershey bar. However, Shorty recognized me and asked me where my bow and arrows were.

"I didn't think you would remember me," I said, and added, "The bow and arrows are safely back at camp. You needn't worry." Shorty nodded approvingly and moved on.

Some time later, the train rolled easily up a long, slight grade and I knew we were approaching the station at Sabattis. I stayed in my seat, although it seemed strange not to be getting off there. Next, the train passed through Tupper Lake Junction, where several passengers disembarked. On the move again, we headed north of the State campsite at Fish Creek Ponds, then on to Lake Clear, where we stopped again. The last leg of the trip was southeast to Saranac Lake, where we stopped at the station just north of the business district. I was pleased to see that I was on time. After asking directions, I found the beauty salon and entered. My tanned face, the blue jeans, and hiking boots gave me a novel appearance not usually seen in a beauty salon. A tall, slim man came forward, looked at me curiously, then asked what I would like.

"I want a haircut, one of the new short bobs," I said. "Outdoor work in the summer is no place for long hair."

"Where do you work? In a nursery or on a farm?"

"Oh, no," I replied, "I climb a mountain every day." That was a conversation starter, and when I told him what I did, he said he thought fire observer work was only for men.

"A lot of men are in service so there's a labor shortage. Anyway, don't I look capable of handling the job?"

"Of course, of course. I just never heard of a woman doing that kind of work," he replied with a grin.

In half an hour, I felt like a new person. I was happy with the way my new haircut set off my features and pleased with how it felt so light and bouncy. All the way back to Nehasane, I relished my new look, and wondered what my friends would say. Mrs. Virgil and Mr. Collier met me at the station. As I stepped off, I could tell that they were sizing up my appearance. I was pleased and relieved when both of them showed their approval with smiles. Mrs. Virgil grasped my hands and said, "Makes you look older, but handsomely so."

"That's so nice of you," I murmured and turned to Mr. Collier with a questioning look.

"I like it, too," he said. "You'll like it even better the next hot day you climb the mountain."

After an early supper at the lodge, I rode my bike back to Green Valley. Tired from my trip, I had no trouble falling asleep.

The first part of July brought fine weather. Day after day, the visibility was excellent, and that meant that views from the tower were unforgettable. The clear air in the valley enhanced the scenery and aroused the artist in me. The scenery near the ponds especially tempted me, but since they were away from the tower, I had no time to paint them. However, all was not peaceful in Green Valley that month. On one dark and gloomy afternoon, I was riding my bike home from the mountain. The cabin was in sight, but I still had a couple of hundred feet to go when I heard a loud, piercing scream, one that sent a chill through me and seemed to electrify the air.

"What on earth was that?" I thought and brought my bike to a sudden stop. It seemed to have come from the hill in back of my cabin where balsam trees grew the thickest. Could it have been a lynx or a panther? What else could scream like that? I wasn't long in deciding what to do. In a burst of speed, I pedaled furiously toward my cabin, jumped off, and ran inside. I slammed the door and locked it. Knowing animals don't like smoke, I quickly built a fire in the woodstove and hoped the smoke would penetrate the woods and drive whatever it was away. All the time I kept thinking that the thousands of acres of forest surrounding Green Valley could harbor animals thought to have been driven from the region many years ago. Whether or not the smoke did the trick, I had no way of telling, but I heard no more of those terrifying screams.

Later that month, when the days were sweet and balmy and the nights warm and full of the crickets' song, another incident occurred. One still night I had trouble getting to sleep. The window near the ceiling was wide open and the night was pitch black. Suddenly I heard heavy breathing outside under the window. I was so frightened that I could scarcely breathe. It was like a nightmare. After what seemed like many minutes, the heavy breathing gradually stopped. I could not relax, not knowing what was outside. Common sense told me it had to be a large animal. Was it a bear? Would it discover my fresh milk and butter at the spring? I worried and could not sleep. In the morning, I found my supplies intact and that, along with a reassuring talk I had with Mrs. Virgil, eased my fears. She explained that what I had heard was, beyond doubt, a bear. Because of the stillness and humidity that night, its labored breathing sounded particularly loud.

Beautiful days brought on beautiful evenings. One evening when the sunset glowed red behind the tall balsams and spruces in the western sky, I took a short bike ride across the tracks and stopped to admire the reflections in the two ponds. Returning to the cabin, I sat on the steps to listen to the vibrant song of that evening charmer, the white-throated sparrow. Across the clearing, its mate answered with a refrain. When the songster flew to the top of a nearby spruce, I remained motionless. Its clear, liquid tones held me spellbound until it ceased singing as darkness settled over Green Valley. It was time to call it a day.

As I started back from the half-moon house behind the cabin with my trusty flashlight, I heard a sound in the underbrush off to my right. Aiming my light there, I froze in my tracks. Not forty feet from me was a large animal, partly hidden in the balsams. Its eyes glowed fiercely in the beam of my light. My first impulse was to flee, but I knew I shouldn't turn and run. Backing off slowly, I kept my light shining in the animal's face. By then, I suspected it was a bear. Then I heard a whimper in the bushes beyond the bear and realized I probably had a mother bear and her cub to contend with. I backed up faster. Suddenly realizing I might trip over something, I turned and dashed around the side of the cabin. Down I went. I had slipped on a stone and landed on my side just as my flashlight gave out. I heard the bear growl. Somehow, I managed to get to my feet and stumble through the doorway. I was safe, but shaking all over.

In cold sweat, I tried to light the lamp. Thinking a cup of tea would calm me, I built a small fire in the stove. Next morning, I called Mrs. Virgil as soon as I reached the tower. After listening attentively to my story about the bear, she sympathized with how frightened I had been and gave me some advice: "Be especially careful about food of all kinds. Never leave crumbs around outside, and keep your food in closed containers. Don't leave any windows open where a bear could smell it. You are lucky to have that window near the ceiling for ventilation."

"Do you think that bear will come back tonight?" I asked.

"It's not likely. Now that the mother bear knows you are there, she won't be back unless she gets awfully hungry, and I doubt that because there is plenty of natural food in the woods this time of year."

Anxiously, I wondered how to bolster my courage. Then I remembered what Mrs. Virgil had told me before, "Make lots of noise. It will scare animals away." She agreed, "When you return to the cabin this afternoon, don't be quiet. Slam the door and rattle the dishes."

"I've got an idea," I told her. "When I go outside tonight I'll bang on a pan with a metal spoon!"

"That should scare anything away," she laughed. My courage and confidence came bounding back, and I worried no more.

The woods around me never failed to interest me. Birds of all kinds attracted my attention, especially if I heard them singing. The lovely songs of warblers, sparrows, and thrushes floated through the woods. During my days in the tower, I used my binoculars to watch different species flying through the spruces below.

Twice I spotted a Blackburnian warbler, enchantingly beautiful both in color and song. I observed several other species I had only seen on the pages of my field guide. One was a black-throated green warbler looking for insects among the spruce tops. Another was a cheerful little singer I had often heard, but never seen. One day, the song was loud and sounded near, so I grabbed the binoculars and cautiously approached the open window. In a moment, I caught a glimpse of it, but when the small bird with a voice that belied his shy manner flew to an exposed limb, I stared in amazement. It was a winter wren. His song delighted me with its enthusiasm and gaiety. Now that I identified it, I noticed several more in the woods around me.

One morning in early summer, I came upon a magnolia warbler near the trail at the foot of the mountain. Its chrome yellow throat and breast streaked with black lines made it easily identifiable. For several days I also heard a black-throated blue warbler, but saw it only once in the thick woods. A pair of hermit thrushes had built their nest beside the trail near the top of the mountain. Every morning as I approached the spot, they fled into the woods, chirping in a timid sort of way. Later I would hear them singing in the lower branches of the spruces. Their song was almost spiritual, well suited to a lonesome place like a mountaintop. On August 2, I saw a bald eagle for the first time. It was a wonderful sight to look down on that majestic bird, as it soared on the wind below the tower room. I was careful not to move as I watched.

As I became acclimated to the days in the tower, I found I was seldom bored. Whether it was scanning the magnificent forests all around, sketching a favorite view, or reading one of the magazines that Mrs. Virgil had sent me, I kept track of all my activities in a little journal. If I wanted some exercise, I would descend the tower and practice my archery. The only thing I missed was someone to talk to, but a phone call now and then made me feel less isolated.

— Six —

“Mount Electra Tower Reporting”

What pleasure I derived from the State’s high-powered binoculars. If anything was indiscernible below me, the powerful 8 x 40 lenses would settle the question. Sometimes it was someone walking on the railroad tracks a mile away in Green Valley or a boat on Witch Hobble Lake in the opposite direction that attracted my attention. Frequently during the summer, I had the opportunity to study the difference between rising smoke—both from trains and buildings—and rising mist from lakes or ponds. On exceptionally clear days, I spent mornings studying the distant hills, mountains, and lakes. I was curious about Albany Mountain, which I had read about years before, and knew was somewhere in the area.

One day in early July, I happened to pass the binoculars across the top of a mountain five miles away on Brandreth Park and saw for the first time a structure that looked like a radio tower and wondered what I had stumbled onto. I decided to call Bill Touhey, the observer on Salmon Lake Mountain, a few miles to the northeast of the mountaintop in question, to see if he could tell me something about it. After checking my map, I was quite sure he could see it, but Bill did not answer, so I finally gave up. I phoned Mr. Collier at the lodge and found that nobody there knew anything about it. Next, I wrote District Ranger Ernest Blue. I wondered if there might be a secret broadcasting station. It could be almost anything, but I was totally unprepared when he informed me that it was an old observation tower and that it was on Albany Mountain, although he confessed that he didn’t know it was still standing.

"Albany Mountain!" I said. "Good Night! I've been looking for it all over the Adirondack Park and here it is right under my nose."

When I finally got in touch with Bill Touhey he told me that the wooden tower on Albany Mountain had been built years before the steel one had been erected on Mount Electra. This was when a big lumbering job was underway on nearby Brandreth Park. With so many men working in the woods, it made sense to put up a fire tower, even if it had to be privately manned.

During August, when section crews cut and burned brush along the railroad tracks as a prevention against fires caused by sparks from the locomotives, I watched the columns of white smoke rise above the trees and ridges as far north as Sabattis Station. As long as the smoke was near the railroad, I wasn't too concerned because I knew that crews patrolled the tracks behind every train and would certainly notice if anything was wrong.

My first fire alert occurred early in the afternoon on August 25, an exceptionally clear day. I had been leisurely scanning the mountains to the east beyond Lake Lila when I spotted smoke rising in long black wisps where I had never seen it before and where I believed there were no buildings or roads. I studied it carefully for several minutes through the binoculars and decided the smoke was coming from behind a small mountain about ten miles away. There were no high mountains nearby that I could use as landmarks. Several hills in the vicinity were all about the same size. This added to my uncertainty when I tried to line up the smoke source on the map.

I tried unsuccessfully to notify the nearest fire warden and, to my dismay, received no answer when I called the lodge on both of the telephones. Nor did I get an answer when I tried the other numbers on the line, including Bill Touhey's. I gave up in disgust and went back to studying the smoke. I knew the lines were working because I had put a call through to the lodge a couple of hours earlier. I concluded that nobody was within earshot of the telephone, so I could only wait and try later.

The smoke continued to rise during the afternoon. I tried calling several more times but without success. I began to think the line might be broken when Mrs. Virgil answered at 4:30. She relayed my message to Bill Black, the ranger at Sabattis, on a separate line. I was at my cabin preparing supper when word came from Ranger Black that no fire had been reported in that section. I was told to keep an eye on it and report in the morning if smoke continued to rise.

At the tower the next morning, I was alarmed to see white puffs rising along with the black smoke from the same location. The great valley that stretched for miles toward the Seward Range was hazy with smoke in the still morning air. My binoculars could not solve the mystery. I was annoyed, anxious, and by now starting to feel angry. All of my backups had deserted me. What would another observer have done, I wondered. I notified Ranger Black again, and he told me that he had been investigating the situation by calling another fire observer nearer the smoke. He had checked the location again and decided I must be seeing smoke from the burning of trash lumber near the lumber mill on Whitney Park, five miles beyond the mountain that obstructed my view. What a relief! It was good to know that I was wrong and that there was no forest fire.

The next day it rained a little after I reached the tower. Fire and smoke were still on my mind, so I decided to call Bill Touhey and tell him about the smoke I had seen. This time he answered, and my first question made him think a moment.

"Where were you when I called yesterday about two o'clock?"

"I must have been down at the cabin getting some fresh drinking water. Why? Did you call?"

"I called half a dozen times because I spotted smoke north of you quite a distance. Didn't you see it in the afternoon?"

"Hell, yes. I saw smoke near Whitney's old lumber mill, but knew what it was. Is that what you saw?"

"But I couldn't see what was behind that small mountain on this side of the smoke. Now I know where that sawmill is located."

Bill laughed and admitted that he knew about my call to Bill Black. He said, "You handled the situation well for a beginner." He then changed the subject and asked if I knew Sandy McDonald's daughter at Brandreth Station.

"No, I haven't met her. What is her name and how far is it to Brandreth?"

"Her name is Dorothy and it's about three miles down the tracks to Brandreth. You'd enjoy the visit and the chance to meet some nice people."

"All right. It would be a pleasant alternative to a lonely afternoon here."

I decided to walk to Brandreth Station the next Sunday afternoon. It was a pleasant day and I let Mrs. Virgil know where I was going. Swinging a light jacket over my shoulder, I set off south down the tracks. The railroad bed was higher than the surrounding area, and as the ties were spaced about a foot apart, I found walking on them difficult. I could not hike along with my usual stride, and the distance seemed endless.

A half-hour into my walk, I heard a train coming up the tracks behind me. I hoped it would be a passenger train, as a freight train would take forever to pass. When it came into view, I saw coach cars behind the locomotive, and was relieved. As I stepped off the roadbed, I nearly turned an ankle hurrying down the rough ground to the edge of the forest. Seeing me, the engineer gave a short toot on the whistle.

The rest of my walk was uneventful until I saw a building ahead not far from the station. It turned out to be the store. A few people were around and one directed me to the front door. A friendly fellow came forward and introduced himself as Sandy McDonald, the proprietor. I told him my name and asked if I could meet his daughter Dorothy. In return, he wanted to know if I was the fire observer at Nehasane. I told him I was and that I had walked down here from my cabin in Green Valley. Just then a blonde woman, several years older than I, came into the room and held out her hand. "I'm Dorothy McDonald, and you are?"

"I'm Frances Boone from Long Lake. I'm working as the fire observer on Mount Electra for the summer."

"Where is Green Valley?" asked Sandy McDonald, "I know Nehasane Park quite well, but I've never heard of Green Valley."

"You probably know it as Partlow, but the bright green of the valley grasses that contrast with the surrounding forest persuaded me that it deserved a more descriptive name."

"Oh, I know Partlow, the old logging headquarters. I like the new name, though. Come sit awhile before you hike back," he said.

I spent a half-hour visiting with the McDonalds and especially enjoyed Dorothy's company. Before I left, Sandy excused himself, saying he had to have a word with the station agent. When he returned, he suggested that it would be a good idea, what with all the lumberjacks sitting around, for the agent to escort me a short distance up the tracks.

As we were leaving, I became aware of several men staring at me, and I was grateful that Mr. Premo, the station agent, was accompanying me. I had hoped to learn something about the old wooden fire tower on Albany Mountain, but I missed my chance when Sandy McDonald left before I could ask him.

— Seven —

Visitors Are Rare

A lot of time spent alone heightened my desire for company, and guests to the tower were always welcome, though Mount Electra wasn't open to the public like most fire towers because it was on private land. However, according to the tower guest book, the number of visitors during my stay exceeded that of prior years. Still, there were very few signatures in it, but they did include Mr. Collier's and those of a couple of Webb family members.

One Sunday morning, I was on duty at the tower when Mrs. Virgil phoned to ask if I would like to have some visitors. I assured her I would, but she wouldn't tell me who would be coming. She announced she had planned a picnic and, at last, I thought I would have some fun. Before my visitors arrived, I took time to scan the surrounding landscape one more time. Soon I heard the unfamiliar sound of voices. Glancing down, I spied one of the Webb's Shelburne terriers ahead of several people making their way slowly along the trail. I recognized Mrs. Virgil, Mr. Collier, and Henry, the Webb's chauffeur, but the two other people I did not know. Mrs. Virgil, red faced and puffing with each step, arrived last. When she saw that I had come halfway down the tower steps, she grinned. I was delighted that she had made the effort to come see me.

"Good for you, Mrs. Virgil. I'm so pleased you made it up the mountain," I said, as I reached for her hand.

"Well, I wanted a look at the view you're always talking about," she said as she sat down on one of the tower's steps, "but you didn't have a bench along the trail to sit on."

Mr. Collier introduced the others in the party. The man and woman I didn't know were friends of the chauffeur and this was the first time they had climbed a real mountain. They were pleased with their efforts, and I wondered to myself how they would take to the climb up the tower. We had our picnic at the foot of the tower and got to know each other better. Afterward, I invited everyone to try my bow and arrows to see if they could hit the target. I did better than the rest and was teased because I had been practicing and they had not.

I invited Henry and his friends up to the tower room to show them the view. Mrs. Virgil said she would go up later with Mr. Collier. Henry's friends hesitated, but I persuaded them to make the ascent. As we started up, they hung onto the iron railings and dared not look down, but Henry showed no fear and preceded me up each flight of stairs. When we entered the tower room, the lady looked frightened and declared she'd never be able to go down. With the trap door closed under their feet, she breathed a sigh of relief.

"Harry," she said to her husband, "weren't you scared when we climbed above the treetops?"

"Oh, a little," Harry admitted with a shrug, "but we now have an adventure to tell our friends about."

Turning to me, the chauffeur asked, "I suppose you think nothing of your daily climb?"

"It took me a week to get used to it," I confessed. "Now I enjoy it."

My guests marveled at the splendid views all around them. I pointed out landmarks I thought would be of interest: Green Valley where they had seen my cabin and the section of railroad tracks leading north to Nehasane Station. Salmon Lake Mountain and Blue Mountain could be seen to the east. Off to the southwest, I pointed out the shining water of Beaver River Flow in the direction of Old Forge, where they said they had once vacationed. Henry enjoyed using the alidade on the map so much that he didn't want to leave. While we were in the tower room, Mr. Collier and Mrs. Virgil climbed part way up the stairs. They reached a point where they were even with some of the treetops, but Mrs. Virgil was getting out of breath.

"This is high enough for me," she said, looking down uneasily.

"Take a look at Green Valley," Mr. Collier said, as he pointed out familiar places to her. "We're a mile away as the crow flies." Turning in the opposite direction, he identified Rock Lake a mile to the south, and the Stillwater of Beaver River Flow that begins at the outlet of Lake Lila. After enjoying the scenery a few minutes, the two of them slowly descended the stairs and waited for us at the foot of the tower. Going down the steps was a trying experience for my lady guest. The men went ahead, but she hung back, looking terrified.

"I can't do it, I just can't," she insisted as she clung to the map table. I leaned over, put my arm around her shoulders, and said gently but firmly, "Come now, you don't want to stay up here alone. Really, there is nothing to it. Just keep your eyes on the stairs."

Finally, common sense came to her rescue, but she insisted that I hang onto her hand until she approached the ground. Everyone laughed as she knelt and kissed the rock under the tower, then told me the job was "all mine!" They stayed a while longer, but because I had no "easy chairs," as Mrs. Virgil put it, they started down the mountain.

On one other occasion at the tower, I heard voices, followed by a clear hello that floated up to me. I looked down to see two young men. "Who are you?" I called out. Without hesitation, one of them identified himself as Franklin Brandreth. I had heard his name through Jim Emerson at Long Lake, for Jim's father, Wallace, had guided the elder Brandreth on fishing and hunting trips. I invited them up, and learned that the other man was a guest staying at Franklin's camp. They had walked up the railroad tracks from Brandreth Station, curious to meet the young woman stationed at the tower.

"How did you know I was here?" I asked.

"Heard about you at the station store. That's where you hear the latest news."

Then I remembered that the McDonalds knew about my tower job.

"Where are you from? I mean, where is your home?" Franklin said.

When I mentioned Long Lake, his face brightened and he asked if I knew Jim Emerson.

"Do I know him? I should say so. He was a classmate of mine in high school."

"How did you land this job?" Franklin's friend asked.

"Well, it's like this," I explained. "I came to Nehasane in 1940 as a waitress, got to know the area and the people, and then the war broke out. This spring there was a labor shortage, but Mr. Collier, the park superintendent, knew I was capable and offered me the job."

"That makes an interesting story," Franklin said, "but don't you get awfully lonesome?"

"I did at first, but I'm used to it now."

"That's amazing," his friend remarked. "You must talk to yourself."

In acquainting them with the landmarks around the region, they were especially interested in those of Brandreth Park. They were amazed and delighted to learn about the old tower on Albany Mountain and studied it intently through the binoculars.

I kept admiring the fringed buckskin jacket Franklin's friend was wearing, when he pulled it off and told me to try it on. Which I did, but found it way too large, so I quickly returned it with a laugh. After more bantering and joking, the pair took their leave. After they had left, I thought about what nice young men they were, but since I was already interested in Howard, I didn't want to appear too friendly.

Not all July days were sunny. A rainy weekend allowed me a few days off, time that I spent at Long Lake. While I was home my brother, Charlie, drove into the yard with a surprise for me. He reached into the pocket of his forest ranger's uniform and pulled out a baby red squirrel half-asleep. Its mother had been killed on the road and the little squirrel was an orphan.

We christened him Squeaky, and Charlie suggested I take him back with me to Green Valley. My mother warmed a saucer of milk and we were gratified to see the little fellow "go after it." She told me to feed him regularly and often and to keep him warm. We fixed up a shoebox with a piece of woolen cloth inside for Squeaky. I made screened windows on each side of it for light and air and put a small pan of water in one corner. This was Squeaky's home until I returned to Nehasane, where, with Mr. Collier's help, I made a circular cage out of a piece of old screen and fastened a small box under the roof for sleeping quarters. In the center of the cage, we fastened an upright branch with bare limbs so the young squirrel could exercise and improve his climbing ability.

Mrs. Virgil liked my pet and soon gained his trust with savory tidbits. After I returned to my cabin, she phoned me regularly to ask how he was doing. He was a constant source of entertainment, but as a baby had to be handled carefully and gently. I fed him pieces of lettuce, dry cereals, some cooked vegetables, and later on, sunflower seeds. When I climbed the mountain each day, I carried Squeaky in his box. As he grew, he became quicker and wilder, yet he delighted in having me play with him. He grew noticeably and soon became discontented within the confines of his cage and box. As a result, I would let him ride on my shoulder on my hike up to the tower.

One day, after I had had him almost a month, Squeaky leapt from his perch on my shoulder and took refuge up a tree along the trail. No amount of coaxing would bring him down. That was the last I saw of him. Although I missed my little squirrel for a long time, I was consoled in realizing that he had gained his rightful freedom.

My younger sister Ethel, on vacation from her job in Syracuse—she did photo tinting—came and spent a few days with me in early August. She had heard about my job in the woods and wanted especially to see a bear, because living in the city, she had not seen one since she was a child. I met her at Nehasane Station one showery afternoon, wearing my rain poncho and sitting on my bike. Ethel was five years younger than I and not as tall, but was pretty with dark, curly hair. We walked down to the lodge to meet Mrs. Virgil, whose Irish wit and good humor captivated her.

"You'll have to wait until Mr. Collier returns to catch a ride to your cabin," Mrs. Virgil said. "He's working with the hired men and won't be home until supper time."

"We could start walking," I said, "but he'd still have to make a trip with Ethel's suitcase."

"Then you must stay for supper," Mrs. Virgil said. "We're having chicken and dumplings." Almost as one, Ethel and I answered, "We'll stay!" and "But you must let us earn our supper! What can we do for you?"

"You can make the ice cream," she said with a twinkle in her eye.

"We used to make it when we were growing up," I told her and Ethel added,

"Sure, we'll try it! Set us up in business."

We followed Mrs. Virgil out onto the porch where she showed us the wooden, hand-cranked freezer stowed away on the back of an old table.

"Chip off a chunk of ice from the block in the top of the icebox," Mrs. Virgil said. "I'll stir up the custard while you're cracking the ice."

It was now three o'clock and I remembered that making ice cream was not something accomplished in half an hour. So we spent the rest of the afternoon taking turns cranking the freezer. After five o'clock, when the men came back, the most delectable strawberry ice cream was ready at last, but we decided it should be a surprise, and hastily covered up the freezer. At the table, we were served a steaming meal of chicken and dumplings together with a heaping bowl of gingered carrots. Then came the surprise. Mrs. Virgil directed the two youngest fellows at the table to go out on the back porch and bring in the dessert.

"Does it take two men to do that?" Mr. Collier asked, looking at Mrs. Virgil in disbelief.

"The girls have made something special," said Mrs. Virgil.

As soon as they took the wraps off the freezer, the young fellows knew that a real treat was coming.

"Ice cream!" they shouted, as they carried the freezer into the kitchen. At the sink, they dug away the crushed ice and rock salt and set the ice cream-filled canister in the middle of the table. Mrs. Virgil gave me the honor of dishing it out. A plate of brownies mysteriously appeared on the table amid many words of praise.

Not being able to restrain myself any longer, I stood up and said, "The praise should go to Mrs. Virgil. She's the star of this whole production!"

Everyone applauded, and the honored lady rose, her face coloring a little, and bowed graciously. Then she explained how the surprise came about.

When the dishes were done, Mrs. Virgil asked Mr. Collier if he would drive Ethel and me to the cabin, and one of the young fellows overheard her. He jumped to his feet and said, "Mr. Collier has had a hard day. Let me take the girls."

Mr. Collier looked surprised, but before he could object, Mrs. Virgil said, "It would be nice if Ted took the girls to their cabin." Turning to Mr. Collier, she added, "You go out on the porch and relax with the men."

"Relax, my eye! I won't be at ease until my truck gets back, and I know the girls are safe in the cabin."

Ted, one of the two fellows who went for the ice cream, promised to be a model chauffeur, and Mr. Collier finally agreed to let him take the truck. When my bike and Ethel's suitcase were loaded in the back, we climbed in beside him, waved good-bye, and started down the road. Along the way, we learned that Ted liked to sing. He had a pleasing voice, and before we knew it, we were singing right along with him. Besides being talented, he knew all the old songs we grew up with. Our voices rang out in the still evening as we rode along.

When we reached Green Valley, the sun was setting through the thinning clouds and it cast long shadows in the lee of the hills.

After Ted unloaded our belongings, we thanked him and told him how much we enjoyed his company. As he turned the truck around to head back, he leaned out the window and said he hoped we could sing together another day. Then he disappeared in a cloud of dust.

As we walked toward the cabin, Ethel said, "What a great time I had at the lodge, and what a wonderful introduction to Nehasane. Now that I know what the social life is like. . . ." She paused and I interjected, "Now, show me the wild and scenic part."

"Something like that. I can't wait to climb the tower," she replied.

The next day Ethel climbed the mountain with me. She hesitated, but only for a second when she saw how high the tower was. After we reached the tower room, she kept reminding me how marvelous the view was, as I scanned the hills for any sign of smoke.

When Ethel finished admiring the scenery, she told me all the news that she brought from home. She admitted her city job had lost its appeal after two years and she also wanted a better paying position. During her stay, we found plenty of time for sisterly talks. Besides our concern about the war, we discussed our futures. Ethel said she might join the Women's Auxiliary of the Coast Guard, or SPARS as it was known, and asked me if I would like to join. I demurred and told her that I had come to enjoy the outdoor life, and that a career as a weather forecaster interested me. I also told her that I would like to be an artist or perhaps an illustrator.

"I don't think you'll have time for both," Ethel said. "You'll have to make up your mind soon."

One afternoon I loaned my bike to Ethel so that she could pick up my mail at the lodge. On her return, she came across two bears at a raspberry patch. The larger one stood up on its hind legs when it heard her coming, but before she could utter a word, both animals fled headlong into the woods. When she returned to the cabin, she told me about the encounter and that she had never pedaled a bike faster in her life! Then she remembered, with a laugh, that even though she had been frightened, she had been lucky because she had seen not one but two bears. When my sister left for home,

I felt she had gained a new appreciation of backcountry living, although she confessed that she missed the modern conveniences of home.

My world became too quiet after my sister left. Peaceful days and glorious evenings that followed could not dispel the loneliness that came over me. But after a few days, the sunsets, the beautifully tinted sky, and the afterglow helped me to better understand and appreciate the natural world around me, and once again I found myself at peace. Sitting on the cabin steps before sundown, I watched several deer quietly browsing as they moved slowly across the clearing. Familiar bird songs drifted into the clearing on the light breezes. I picked out a robin's calling-for-rain song, a far-off crow's cry, and the lilting song of the white-throated sparrow.

That summer the Bureau of Geodetic Survey out of Albany began work in the Adirondacks. One of their duties was to relay electric light signals from one mountaintop to another at night to check the accuracy of their readings.

In August, one of their parties arrived at Green Valley with all kinds of paraphernalia. I first saw them from the tower as they walked along the railroad tracks toward a small mountain less than two miles away. It was known locally as Baldy Mountain because so much of its summit was bare rock. There they set up a wooden platform on which they placed powerful spotlights. My cabin faced Baldy, and when it became dark, I could see their bright lights flashing messages in Morse code. I found it all fascinating.

Some nights the surveyors encountered bad weather—either heavy haze or unexpected showers. I became interested in learning Morse code and talked with some of the men about it when I saw them on the road. They offered me a booklet to study, and one evening they gave me my first lesson in code signaling by sending me a few simple messages. I found that I could read some of the letters flashed to me, but as the signals came faster than I could figure out the words, I knew I'd better sign off. I had learned to say "good night" and was gratified when I realized that they understood me. I used an ordinary flashlight and found it fun until I couldn't figure out what they were saying.

That same month, on my infrequent trips to the lodge, I kept an eye on the raspberry bushes along the road. The berries were plentiful but not quite ripe. The following week, I spotted one particular patch that looked especially enticing. Ripe raspberries hung from the tall canes and I found that they were delicious. I knew I should return shortly or I would find over-ripe berries dropped to the ground.

The next evening, after a hurried supper, I rode back to the raspberry patch. I parked my bike, turning it around to face the cabin half a mile away, to make sure I could leave quickly, knowing that bears are fond of berries. I placed a rock on the edge of the road and rested the bike's kickstand on it. Soon I was happily picking berries, but saw that they were more plentiful farther from the road. I followed a deer path, nervously looking and listening, lest there be a bear up ahead. Relieved at finding I was alone I started picking again.

The saucepan I had brought with me was nearly full when I heard a fierce growl.

On the way to the cabin with my mail, Mr. Collier and a friend spotted my bicycle beside the berry patch and quietly approached me. Coming to a stop, they could see I was busy picking berries and hadn't seen or heard them yet. Mr. Collier decided to have some fun and gave a bear-like growl. Hearing it, I let out a shriek and jumped up. As I did so, my container of berries, which I had just raised to clear a large log, tipped over. As I whirled to face the direction the noise came from, several berries fell under my blouse. Only then did I see Mr. Collier and his friend laughing. I glared at them.

"You made me lose all those berries!"

Sensing my anger, Mr. Collier apologized and told me he had some mail for me. The prospect of mail made me forget about the spilled berries.

"I'll leave the bundle behind the screen door at the cabin. We're going on to Partlow Lake," he called out as he left.

The fire tower on Mount Electra was 70 feet high. Photographed in 1942.

The author when Howard Seaman "looked her up" at Long Lake in 1940.

Howard plows the road near Nehasane Station in 1941.

Pond beside the road near the trail leading up Mount Electra in 1942.

The author with Mr. Collier's cocker spaniel.

At the author's cabin in Green Valley. She has just returned from the lodge where she picked up fresh milk and her mail pouch.

The author's favorite pond. She passed it every day on her way to work at the tower.

The author at archery practice below the base of the tower.

The author at Forest Lodge showing off her new short hair-do after her trip to the beauty salon in Saranac Lake.

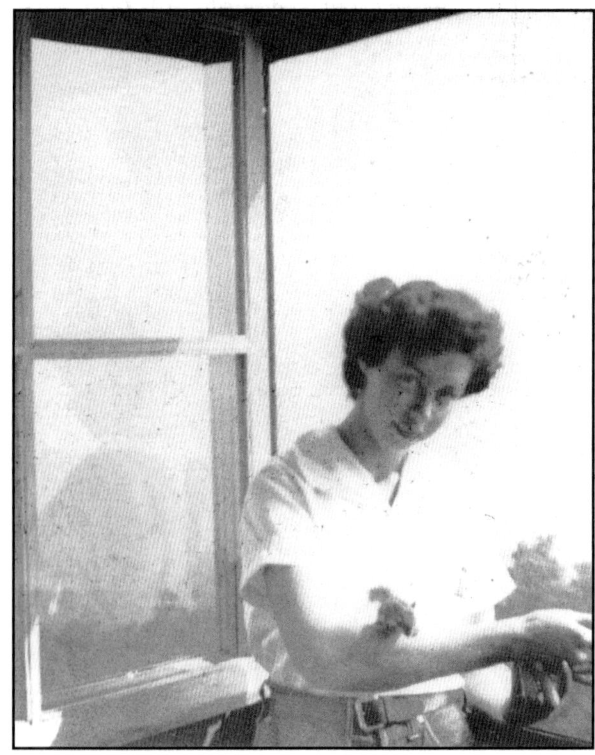

The author at the tower with Squeaky, her pet squirrel.

Camp at Gull Lake when it was new. Photograph by T.E. Marr, 1890s.

Courtesy Adirondack Museum

Looking northeast from Mount Frederica over Lake Lila.

Looking back along the trail from halfway up the tower. It was from here that the author, close to the end of her days at the tower, saw Howard depart for the last time.

When I returned to the cabin, I found a packet of letters held together by a large rubber band behind the screen door. I was delighted to see that one was from Howard with the now-familiar Langley Field postmark. Others were from my dad, my sister in Schenectady, and a friend in Maine. My letter writing had finally paid off, and reading and rereading them gave me an evening of pleasure.

— Eight —

The Nature of Things

As August and the remaining days of summer slipped by, fewer deer came to the salt lick in the clearing at Green Valley. Heavy morning fogs over the lakes still had not lifted by the time I reached the top of the mountain. I always enjoyed seeing this. To me it was one of nature's signals for a beautiful day free of storm clouds and wind. On these days, when one could see to the horizon, I spent hours with my binoculars, fascinated by the grandeur and beauty of the highest peaks in the Adirondacks. Their distant forms appeared soft blue, yet I was able to recognize some by their distinctive shapes. As a mountain climber, I felt an affinity for them.

Again and again, the views from the tower challenged me to try to capture them on paper or canvas. My first attempt was a pencil drawing on a narrow, three-foot-long sheet of heavy paper that showed the view from the north and east windows. It took in Green Valley with the handsome little ponds near the road, and the rolling hills beyond, including the side of Mount Frederica overlooking Lake Lila. The lake was hidden, but I was able to include snatches of other lakes in the distance. Near the horizon, I sketched in the faint shapes of the High Peaks far to the northeast. One day I showed the finished drawing to Mr. Webb at the lodge and he talked me into giving it to him, much as I hated to part with it. He said something about getting it framed, but I never knew what became of it.

With my watercolors, I painted a larger picture of the south view showing Rock Lake and the Stillwater of Beaver River Flow. The table in the center of the tower room made an ideal place to work. I worked with watercolors on half a dozen sunny days, and the rendering took shape quickly. I depicted Rock Lake prominently in the middle distance, with several old virgin pines guarding its shores. I managed to keep this painting, and it became a treasured souvenir of my summer in the tower.

By the middle of August, the woods had become increasingly dry, and that meant I had to be extra vigilant at the tower. I no longer had time for reading or archery practice on the job, and the dry weather, I discovered, also brought out hordes of crickets and grasshoppers. There was no lack of them around, and even inside, my cabin. On warm evenings, the crickets serenaded me, sometimes keeping me awake well into the night. And on my bike trips back and forth to the lodge, flickers became a common sight along the side of the road. Seeing me, they would flee with their characteristic bounding flight. With their spotted tan and gold plumage and the red patch at the back of their heads they were easy to recognize.

I was thankful that I had seen nothing of the bears lately, and as my confidence grew, I felt that I would be able to handle almost any chance meeting. The early summer had been wet and warm enough to provide plenty of wild berries so I was sure that bears would not be hungry enough to bother me.

One afternoon, with the sky clear after a morning rain, I felt adventurous and decided to explore beyond Green Valley. After descending Mount Electra, I climbed on my bicycle and headed west along the winding road to Partlow Lake, a road that led into higher hills and heavier forest growth. Occasionally I would see the flash of a white flag, a signal that told me that deer were feeding near the road and that I had scared them away. I found riding invigorating as the wind tugged at my hair and cooled my flushed face. Soon I was coasting rapidly downhill.

The road ahead disappeared around a curve to the left, and as I swung around it, I saw a black form in the middle of the road. It was a young bear cub, just as startled as I was, and it looked tensed for flight. Instantly, I realized that the mother bear must be nearby. My heart was in my throat. What if I hit the cub? I yelled and braked enough to skid the rear wheel to make more noise, and whirled by along the shoulder of the road. The cub dashed into the brush, but the mother bear appeared and lit out after me! I heard her bawl angrily and that spurred me to pedal even faster.

After traveling a hundred yards, I anxiously glanced over my shoulder. I thanked the Lord when I saw the big bear turn aside and give up the chase. I did not stop for another quarter of a mile. By then, I was weak and tired. I stopped, dropped the bicycle, and sat down on a log beside the road. My clothes felt clammy and I was trembling. The peace and quiet of my resting place brought me slowly back to reality. I felt safe here.

Then a fearful thought crossed my mind, "How would I get back to my cabin?" I certainly didn't want to return the way I had come and chance another meeting with that irate bear. I wished that I knew more about the roads in the park. Maybe there was an alternate route back. Perhaps I could find one at Partlow Lake.

Farther along, as I walked the bike up an easy grade, I heard a vehicle approaching. As it came into sight, the driver slowed down when he saw me. At that moment, I didn't care who it was. The truck stopped beside me and I recognized Mr. Collier, although I didn't know the well-dressed fellow with him.

"Are you lost?" Mr. Collier asked. "And why aren't you riding?"

"I had a close call with an angry mother bear, back about a quarter of a mile."

When I finished telling about my encounter, the other man let out a low whistle as he looked at me. Mr. Collier then introduced him as Ed Steen, the one who would take his place for a week while he was away on business.

"I guess you'd do well to ride back with us," said Mr. Collier as he alighted and placed my bike in the rear of the truck. I didn't argue. Ed Steen got out of the front seat and climbed into the back so that I could ride with Mr. Collier.

"This has been my lucky day. First, I escaped that bear, then you came along just when I needed a ride. I don't know how I would have made it back alone to my cabin."

"It would have been risky. That old bear has your scent," said Mr. Collier.

"Yes, it's pretty fresh in her mind!" joked Ed Steen, who heard me through the open window.

"It's pretty fresh in my mind, too!" I said as we started home.

Not long afterwards, Mr. Collier spoke up and pointed. "There's where the bear chased you. See how the dirt is torn up."

"Good grief. I hope those bears aren't still near here!"

Then Ed Steen said, "There they are! They're messing around that old tree stump." He pointed into the woods where we saw two bears in a small clearing. The big one was clawing at the tree stump, then frantically jumping around, while the cub kept its distance.

"They've found a bee tree!" exclaimed Mr. Collier, "And they're after the honey." We watched their antics for a few minutes, and then headed home.

After that exciting and exhausting day, I slept well, and next day was ready to enjoy the peace and beauty of the tower once again.

That morning, Bill Touhey phoned me from the Salmon Lake Mountain fire tower.

"Say, Frances, can you see blue smoke south of here, and east of your tower? It looks to be about five miles from you. Maybe it's on Brandreth Park."

"Then it's behind Partlow Hill, where I can't see," I replied.

"All right, I'll keep an eye on it."

The next day I called Bill about the smoke, and he told me that campers at North Pond near Brandreth Lake had caused it. He had checked it out by calling the people at Brandreth.

A couple days later, a terrible thunderstorm swept over the mountains. Its fury, I thought, set the record for the summer. It came up quickly about six o'clock, after I had left the mountain. I had a twenty-minute warning of its approach by the sound of thunder coming ever nearer. I was preparing my supper when the storm broke with a suddenness that frightened me. High winds accompanied terrific bolts of lightning and claps of thunder that crashed all around the valley. One fearful bang shook the cabin and a blinding flash of lightning flooded the room. I slammed the door shut, yanked down the telephone switch over the sink, and jumped on the bed where I stayed and prayed.

The cabin became darker by the minute and the rain flew in through the open window over the table. I didn't dare try to close it. Several times, lightning exploded with a terrifying crack at the switch above the sink, so I knew the telephone was out of order. Every time I attempted to leave the bed, another flash of lightning changed my mind.

Finally, the storm passed. The sky brightened and the air became cooler. When I finally sat down to my supper, I realized that I was starved. It was as though I had not eaten all day. I had made a hearty stew of lamb and vegetables, which had been starting to simmer when the storm hit. Now the fire was nearly out. I restarted it with a few sticks of kindling and added half a bay leaf and a cut-up onion to the stew. A savory aroma soon filled the cabin. With a couple of Mrs. Virgil's homemade rolls added to my plate, I found it a great pleasure to partake of a special meal after such an uproar.

The storm left chaos in its wake. The next morning, since my telephone was not working, I scouted up the road toward Forest Lodge. I found one tree leaning across the wires, and then another one near the road that had disrupted my telephone service. I wondered what I would find on the mountain trail. But a couple days would pass before I could find out, because the area at the beginning of the trail was flooded, and the road near the bridge was under water. Later in the afternoon, Mr. Collier arrived at the cabin and asked how I had weathered the storm.

"It gave me quite a scare," I admitted, "and the lightning was too close for comfort."

"I can imagine," he replied, "It was close at the lodge too. We couldn't call you, so I knew a tree was down on the line. Ed was with me this morning and we cleared away a couple that fell on the lines and repaired the damage. Have you been up on the mountain yet?"

"No, the trail in the valley was flooded," I said. "I'll try tomorrow."

"Check the lines, and if you find a problem, call us."

The next morning was drier when I started out for the tower. The high water had drained off enough to let me walk along the base of the mountain. Limbs and debris littered the path, and I looked for but saw no sign of Nanny. Near the spring, a section of a rotted tree had pulled the telephone line to the ground. I rolled it off and freed the wire. Farther up the trail, a large balsam tree had come down across the trail and the line. This was a job for Mr. Collier. Going around this barrier, I proceeded up the trail to the tower. Near the top of the mountain, I came across another fallen tree that had pinned the telephone wire to the ground. I realized then that it might take a couple of days to repair the tower phone service, but I didn't need to worry about watching for fire.

Out of habit, I kicked aside branches that had come down during the storm. Reaching the tower, I found that one window had come unfastened by the wind but was not broken. I surveyed my domain to see that all was well, and then returned to the cabin and called Mr. Collier.

"There are two trees lying across the line up the mountain," I reported. "One is a large balsam about half way up and the other is a dead birch tree near the top."

"We'll be there tomorrow to start clearing them away," Mr. Collier said.

"Would you mind clearing the branches off the trail as you go up? That will help us and save time later."

I agreed, and left the cabin a bit earlier than usual the next morning. At the foot of the mountain, as I was picking up branches, I saw Nanny coming toward me. She came close enough to see if what I was picking up was something to eat. Opening my knapsack, I found a stale crust of bread that broke into pieces as she took it out of my hand. Leaving her behind, I made my way slowly up the trail tossing aside branches as I went. Later in the morning, I heard the sound of axes and chainsaws down on the trail. By noon, they had finished clearing away the dead birch near the summit and had reached the base of the tower. I joined them for lunch on the tower steps.

"Do you think the telephones will work now?"

"We're not sure, but they should be all right," Mr. Collier said. "I'll try them out before we leave."

"If they don't work, you'll have to send your messages by Morse code," Ed Steen teased. I knew then that he had heard about my efforts to learn the code.

"Who would I send them to? Bill Touhey? He's the only one around who could see my signals."

With lunch finished, Mr. Collier climbed the tower and called the lodge. Mrs. Virgil answered, and said how glad she was to know the line was working again.

When the men were ready to leave the mountain top, Mr. Collier said, "I'll be away next week, and Ed will be in charge while I'm gone. He knows the routine at the lodge. Do you have any questions?"

"None. Thank you both for a job well done! Now I'm going to try out the phones, and call Bill."

Soon they were on their way, and I returned to the tower room. I checked the surrounding forests once more with the binoculars before calling Bill Touhey. I wasn't surprised to find his line dead, which I knew meant that the telephone line was damaged between us. In a few days, I phoned Bill again and was relieved to hear his gruff voice. He told me that he had had a close call during the storm when lightning struck a tall tree between the tower and his cabin just as he walked in the door.

— Nine —

Tribulation

On the morning of August 24, when I stepped out of the cabin, I saw frost on the ground for the first time. I had neglected to cover my flowerbeds and my nasturtiums lay blackened and wilted along the path. Later that day, after returning from the mountain, I cleaned up the sad looking plants before anyone else saw them.

In late summer, different birds took their turn visiting the mountaintop. Yellow-bellied sapsuckers often surprised me with their sudden hammering on the steel frame of the tower. Their tapping amused me and I thought it sounded like Morse code. I burst out laughing at those silly birds, and at myself when I hurried to look.

A few days later, I saw that many of my old friends on their way south had stopped. The spruce trees were full of birds. I recognized a Blackburnian warbler by his flashy orange breast and sweet, chirping song. A golden-crowned kinglet was busy in the lower branches while a female redstart, flaunting her yellow-barred tail, was chasing her neighbors.

Shortly after the day of the first frost, Mr. Collier left Nehasane on a business trip to the city. Mrs. Virgil gave me the news when I called in from the tower.

"He left on the morning train, and Ed Steen saw him off at the station," she said.

"Will Ed drop off my groceries like Mr. Collier did?"

"I'm sure he will. Do you have an order ready? I'll be sending mine out tomorrow, so let me know."

A couple of days after Mr. Collier's departure, I noticed the sky becoming overcast as I climbed the mountain. By midmorning, the sun had disappeared and by noon the rain began falling in misty veils. After closing the windows, I decided to stay at the tower until it stopped and then, if there was no lightning, return to my cabin. After eating my lunch, I sat down to read a chapter of Zane Grey's *Riders of the Purple Sage.*

I forgot about the rain and never suspected anything was wrong until my feet felt wet. Looking down, I saw that water covered the floor. My chair was surrounded. Rain had leaked in around the poorly sealed windows. I grabbed an old whiskbroom from under the table and swept the water into the cracks around the trapdoor. Looking out, I was amazed that I could see only as far as the tops of the nearby trees. The hills and mountains had vanished, and low, heavy clouds swept around the tower. An eerie feeling came over me. It was like being adrift in a boat.

By three o'clock, the storm had let up and the rain had stopped. I saw no reason to remain at the tower so I decided to leave the mountain. When I called Mrs. Virgil at the lodge, she said there was some mail for me, including a letter from Howard. This news lifted my spirits and I gathered up my belongings and disconnected the telephone. I wondered vaguely if Ed Steen would bring my mail or should I ride to the lodge and collect it.

As I left the tower room, I let the trap door down with a bang and started down the steps. I felt excited and wondered what news Howard's letter might bring. Hurrying down the steps, I failed to realize the landings were still wet from the rain. As I swung around a landing halfway down, I slipped on a wet leaf. Losing my footing, I went down with a terrible thump, and skidded into a corner of the landing. My legs slid over the edge and hung out into space. Frantically, I grabbed a steel strut.

"Oh, God, help me!" I cried out when I realized what had happened. The fall had temporarily paralyzed me, and it was another minute before I could command enough strength to pull myself back from the edge. I had landed partly on my left side and back, and found myself looking up at the sky. When I tried to move, I felt pain in my hip, and I knew my leg had scraped against something when I went down. Reaching back over my head, I felt the bottom of the step above me and pulled myself farther back. Every move made me wince, and I wondered, as I began to feel faint, how badly I was hurt.

After some minutes, I was able to turn and bring my feet to rest on the step below. I knew then that my hip was not broken, only badly bruised. But I was shaken and scared. My knapsack, I saw, had dropped to the ground thirty feet below me. I would have to get back to the cabin as best I could. Pulling myself together and gingerly getting on my feet, I slowly descended to the base of the tower.

Going down the mountain trail was torture, and I wished somehow that I could fly. Common sense told me I shouldn't be walking, but I had no choice. By moving very slowly and resting every few feet, I finally reached the bottom of the trail. I felt miserable and wished I had something for the pain. Continuing on, I came in sight of the road. In too much pain to ride my bike, I left it where I had parked it that morning.

It was seven o'clock by the time I reached the cabin. After washing my hands, I went to work on my scrapes and bruises. The side of my leg burned. It was raw and looked worse than I expected. I worried about it getting infected, and on the long walk back to my cabin, I had done some serious thinking about first aid. I had no Merthiolate; the only first-aid kit was at the tower. Then I remembered what my mother had told me about using herbs for healing. For centuries when there was nothing else available, she said, people had used raw potato to treat bruises. She had also told me about aloe vera, a plant with excellent healing qualities. This I knew from first-hand experience with burns. Luckily, I had brought a small plant with me from home, and anxious to give it a try, I broke off a thick leaf and spread the healing gel on the red scrapes of my leg. For my bruised hip, I taped on a compress of a handkerchief folded over pieces of thinly sliced potato.

When I had finished, I realized how hungry I was, but I felt so weak and "achy" that all I could do was lie down—very carefully—on the bed. Not long afterward, I heard the sound of a vehicle stopping in my yard. I heard voices, and guessed it had to be someone from the lodge with my mail.

Muttering under my breath, I tried painfully to stand up. They knocked and, hearing my voice, opened the door and came in. It was Mrs. Virgil and Ed Steen. One look at me and they knew something was wrong. Mrs. Virgil came to me as I sank back onto the bed, and Ed, after tossing the mail on the table, asked if I was sick.

"Not sick, just banged up," I said trying to be nonchalant or brave, I didn't know which.

"What happened?" Mrs. Virgil said as she sat down beside me.

"I slipped and fell going down the tower steps," I began slowly and described my fall hesitatingly. By the time I had finished, Ed Steen decided I should see a doctor, and Mrs. Virgil insisted that I return with them to the lodge to stay overnight. When she heard that I had not eaten since noon, she said, "There is plenty to eat in my pantry, so come along with us."

She didn't need to ask twice. Her offer sounded so good, that I accepted gratefully.

Ed Steen noticed that my bike was missing and asked me if it was over at the trail. I told him it was and he left to retrieve it. By the time he returned and put the bike inside the cabin, Mrs. Virgil had my suitcase packed, and we were ready to return to the lodge. I spent the next few days recuperating. It was like a vacation, except I was so lame and sore I could hardly get around. Mrs. Virgil's medicine cabinet held remedies that were more up-to-date than those I had used, so I was thankful when she patched me up her way. I spent much of each day in an easy chair in the kitchen. As Ed said, "It hurts me as much as it does you, every time I see you trying to get up." Mrs. Virgil agreed and said she hoped I'd be a lot more careful in the future.

When I was alone, I thought about my mail, which I had inadvertently left on the table at the cabin. I hoped that I could return to the cabin the next day and therefore I waited patiently. Rainy weather set in on the second day, and that eased my conscience about not being on duty at the tower. On the fourth day, I felt well enough to return to Green Valley. As I said good-bye, I gave Mrs. Virgil a hug. "I don't know what I would have done without you!" I said as tears came to my eyes.

After putting fresh groceries and a loaf of Mrs. Virgil's home-baked bread in the truck, Ed Steen drove me back to the cabin. When we reached the clearing, I thought that it looked like such a lonely place. This was something I had not felt since my first week there. While I was busy with my suitcase, Ed carried in the box of groceries and I said to him, "This place seems lonesome and dull. It can't be the weather because the sun is shining."

"No, it's not the weather. You got spoiled at the lodge, what with everybody waiting on you."

"So you think being spoiled is my problem?" I asked.

"Of course. As soon as you start thinking about that view from the tower or the letter from your boyfriend, you'll be fine."

After Ed left, I picked up the letters on the table, and looked for Howard's handwriting. I found the envelope and saw that it was postmarked over a week ago. Reading his letter, I suddenly realized what he had written. He's coming home on furlough in another week. I looked at the calendar on the wall. That will be a week from this Saturday. I sank into a chair.

Still holding the letter, I read the last sentence again. "Plan on coming home for a couple days. I can't wait to see you. Love, Howard."

— Ten —

Days That Make the Heart Sing

The excitement I felt from Howard's letter lasted all week. I passed along the good news that he was coming to Mrs. Virgil and Bill Touhey and even to Pete Wood's family. Both Mrs. Virgil and Mr. Collier had liked Howard ever since he had first come to work at Nehasane Park. Because I was looking forward to having some time off, Mrs. Virgil jokingly said, "It better rain next weekend or you can't go."

"I'll pray for rain," I answered, then asked, "When will Mr. Collier return?"

"He should be back in a couple days," she replied.

I told my parents and a few friends in Long Lake that Howard was coming. They knew him slightly, because he had grown up in town. As fast as mail could travel, I heard back from my dad that they would be happy to see me anytime, and my friend was welcome, too.

The rest of the week passed quickly. I had another visitor at the tower midweek when Bill Black, the forest ranger, came to see Mount Electra and its tower. He recalled the conversation we had had two weeks earlier when I reported the smoke. Bill had been an observer on West Mountain near Raquette Lake. While I studied that mountain with the binoculars, he told me about the time he had located and reported a fire from its tower. I also learned about other fire towers on adjacent mountains. Bill said that he had visited every tower in sight, but this was his first ascent of Mount Electra.

Mr. Collier returned before the end of the week, and Ed Steen regretfully left Nehasane and returned home. When Mr. Collier learned of my fall, he called to ask about it. I assured him I was in good shape and intended to stay that way. Finally, the day I had been waiting for arrived. Mrs. Virgil received a telephone message from Howard saying he was at Long Lake, and wanted to know when I could get some time off. Luckily, the weather had been wet, and after Mrs. Virgil called, I talked with Mr. Collier who arranged for me to have a few days off.

"Mrs. Virgil and I want to see Howard too. Why doesn't he join you on your return trip?"

"Oh! I'm sure he would like that," I replied.

"Then I'll make out two passes for the station stop."

"I'd leave tomorrow, if I may," I said. "There was a good rain yesterday."

Mrs. Virgil then phoned Howard, and I received word back from her that he would meet me the next day at Sabattis Station on the morning train.

The following morning, after spending the night at the lodge, I boarded the train that Mr. Collier flagged down for me.

"Have a safe trip," he said as I climbed aboard, "and let me know the day and time you'll return."

Since the country was at war, I wasn't surprised to see a couple of young men in uniform sitting up front in the coach. I wondered if Howard would be wearing his uniform. How would he look with a crew cut? These thoughts kept me occupied, but the train seemed to take forever to pass the familiar landmarks I knew along the way. Soon the whistle blew for the stop at Sabattis. As I gathered up my belongings, I felt a tingle of excitement. Alighting with other passengers, my gaze searched the group of people near the station door. A tall young man in uniform came toward me. He had a broad smile, and I only had time to say his name before he wrapped me in a big hug.

"Stand back and let me look at you," he said. "You're even better looking than the last time I saw you."

"And so are you, Howard Seaman. Especially in that uniform," I replied. "You must be a sergeant. Am I right?"

"I'm just a cog in Uncle Sam's army," he answered with a grin, as he picked up my luggage. "How's everything at Nehasane?"

"Couldn't be better. Your friends at the lodge said to say hello."

"That's nice. I'd like to see them."

"Maybe you will."

We walked through the station and out the door to where several cars were parked.

"Is that your faithful old Ford?" I asked when I recognized it.

"That's my old jitney, and she'll have to do until the war is over."

The drive home was on a winding macadam road through nineteen miles of beautiful forest, but we were so interested in each other and on catching up with all the news that we scarcely noticed the scenery. Yet, when we reached Long Lake, Howard began looking at all the places he remembered, and remarked on the changes he noticed. As we started up Newcomb Road from the intersection, Howard suddenly thought of something, and said, "Your folks are expecting us for lunch and I promised to get you there on time."

"Oh, how nice. This is the best homecoming I can remember. I'm so glad that you're here to enjoy it." For that remark, I got a surprise handclasp that made me giggle. When we drove into my parents' yard, Howard blew the horn. The front door opened and my brother Bill, followed by my mother and dad, came out to greet us.

This was the beginning of three memorable days. Howard and I went canoeing, hiked the Northville–Placid trail to the First Brook, swam in Lake Eaton, went out to dinner, and saw a movie at Becker's Theater. I even got to church on Sunday, and that pleased my folks. At Howard's family's house, only his sisters and a younger brother were home. We spent an evening with them and I'll never forget the fun we had. I learned how to make chocolate fudge from his oldest sister who was a good cook. But we both had Howard to contend with. He teased us constantly. If it wasn't the sack of sugar that disappeared, it was the chocolate. The evening was saved from further trouble when we settled down to look at the family photo album until the fudge was cool enough to eat.

The night we went out to dinner, I told Howard that he had an invitation to visit Nehasane and could accompany me on my return. That pleased him immensely, and when I told him that both Mr. Collier and Mrs. Virgil hoped to see him, he was elated.

All too soon it was time to contact Mr. Collier at the lodge for the return trip. The weather had been pleasant, but turned hot the afternoon of our departure. Howard changed from his uniform to civilian clothes because, he joked, he didn't want to spoil his uniform if he should be caught in another rain storm with me. After the train left Sabattis, the sky darkened ominously. Before we reached Nehasane, lightning flashed and thunder crashed in the hills. It was pouring rain by the time we reached the station. Howard turned to me and asked, "Do you remember the time we got caught in a downpour once before?"

"Oh, yes! What a sight we were. But it was a good omen. We've liked each other ever since."

We spotted Mr. Collier's truck parked near the station house. He stood in the doorway and beckoned to us. Howard grabbed the luggage and my hand, and by running as fast as we could, the rain only dampened our clothing. Mr. Collier shook Howard's hand and said how pleased he was to see him again and Howard reciprocated by thanking Mr. Collier for the invitation. Meanwhile, Pete and Rose welcomed me back, and after Pete greeted Howard, he settled back in his office chair, and said, "Just like old times having both of you here again."

"I wish I could stay longer," Howard said, "but I must take the train back tomorrow afternoon."

"Where is Mrs. Virgil?"

"She's at the lodge," said Mr. Collier, and added, "The rain has let up. Let's go."

We found Mrs. Virgil waiting in the kitchen. She greeted Howard who gave her a special hug.

"My goodness! You're a sight for sore eyes. How about it, Frances?"

"Of course," I said, "but you should see him in his uniform!"

With that, the men sauntered into the men's sitting room for a short visit. Mrs. Virgil had supper started, so I set the table as I visited with her. Later, our hosts decided that Howard and I should stay at the lodge overnight, and set out for the mountain in the forenoon.

The next day was sunny. At breakfast, we discussed our plans for the day. Howard wanted to climb Mount Electra and be with me for one more day. Mr. Collier decided to let Howard borrow the truck, as he would have to be back by afternoon to catch the train. When we left the lodge, we picked up my mail and fresh groceries and the lunch that Mrs. Virgil had put together for us. Soon we were on our way. Howard said he hoped we'd see some wildlife, and before long we came across several deer feeding beside the road.

"So you finally saw some bears, eh?" Howard asked, and looked at me keenly, as he recalled what I had told him about my close call on the bicycle.

"No more bears for me." I then laughed and added, "Seeing bears can be your priority."

When we reached the clearing, I showed Howard my rustic summer home.

"Pretty nice setup you have here," he said approvingly. "It's a good thing you have a cold spring not far from the cabin, otherwise where would you keep your perishables?"

We soon crossed Green Valley, and Howard remarked on the beauty of the ponds. At the trail, he wanted to know when we could expect to see Nanny, my pet deer. I remembered I had no bread in my knapsack and, if she appeared, I would have to share my sandwich with her.

"We should see her at the beginning of the trail up the mountain. If not, I'll try calling her."

Nanny soon appeared, but refused to come near me when she saw Howard. At the spring, a third of the way up the mountain, I rinsed out the glass jug, and half filled it with fresh water. The climb warmed us up, and we took our jackets off. At the top of the trail, we paused to rest and Howard asked, as I had many weeks before, "Where is the tower?"

"At the middle of this ridge, behind the treetops." Remembering my own confusion, I added, "Wait till you see how high it is."

Howard walked along the trail ahead of me, anxious for a look. Suddenly, he stopped and motioned for me to stay back. What did he see? After a minute, he walked quickly toward me. "A mother bear and her cub were on the first landing of the tower stairs. They were looking over your premises." He laughed softly and continued, "They left in a hurry, when one of them saw me on the trail."

"They knew I was away for a few days, and came to have a look around. Anyway, you have seen your bears. Are you sure they're gone?"

"I'm quite sure," he answered as we walked over to the base of the tower.

Looking up, he glanced at me and grinned, "Why did they give you such a high one?"

"To test my grit, of course."

"O.K., sweetie, lead the way. I want to see that view."

We walked up the flights of stairs without stopping, and both of us were out of breath by the time we reached the top.

"You didn't give me any chance to look at the view," Howard said as he helped me raise the trapdoor.

"It's best up in the tower room. You'll see," I said as we climbed up and dropped the trap door in place.

Looking around, Howard slowly took in all 360 degrees of the scenery.

"You weren't exaggerating." he exclaimed and, looking at the map, began to identify the bodies of water below us.

It was a pleasant noon hour. After I had scanned the landscape, Howard used the alidade and the binoculars as he explored the points of interest with me. Suddenly, I realized we hadn't called our friends at the lodge. I rang the number and gave the receiver to Howard.

His enthusiastic tone told me, as well as Mrs. Virgil, how much he was enjoying himself. We then sat down to savor our lunch. All too soon, it was time for Howard to leave. He seemed impressed by my job as observer, and turning to me, held my shoulders at arm's length and said, "I've got to hand it to you, lady. You're perfect for this job."

I blushed. Praise like that was new to me. The hug he gave me brought back my smile.

He looked at his watch and said, "It's time for me to hit the trail, and it is a long trail back. I've sure enjoyed seeing you and being at Nehasane again."

"Write to me when you get back to the base," I entreated. And he promised he would.

I followed Howard down the many flights of stairs. Then arm in arm we walked to the beginning of the trail down the mountain where I bid him farewell. A lingering kiss, a tight handclasp, and he was on his way. I wanted to run after him, but instead called out a last good-bye. Turning around, Howard raised his cap and smiled at me. Then he disappeared among the trees. Lost in reverie, I slowly climbed back up the stairs. Stopping now and then on a landing, I realized my vacation was over.

— Eleven —

The Last Days on the Mountain

By the middle of September, a few days after Howard's departure, the golden hand of autumn reached into the Adirondacks and touched Nehasane Park. The cold nights started to work their magic, and that week the maples were among the first to flaunt their colors. Soon these hills became such an inspiring sight from the top of my mountain that I wished the whole world could see them.

On the trail, I found myself hiking through an ever-deeper layer of leaves that rustled noisily as I moved through them. Chipmunks, popping in and out of their holes at my approach, seemed busier than ever. Some waited until I was only a few feet away before sounding the alarm and dropping out of sight. Others I saw were laying away a store of beechnuts for the winter, and most had their cheeks filled to capacity.

On September 22, I ascended Mount Electra twice within two hours. The second occasion was prompted by the arrival at Nehasane of Ernest Blue, the district forest ranger. I had been expecting him all summer, having been told that he would come to inspect telephone lines and connections, but now that September was drawing to a close, I had given up hope of meeting him.

On that sunny morning, I had barely unlocked the tower and turned the telephone switches on when Mr. Collier called from the cabin. He had Mr. Blue and a fire warden named McEdwards with him. Then came the disappointing news that they weren't coming up the mountain. Instead, he asked that I come down and meet them on the road in an hour. By then, they would have returned from an inspection of the telephone lines on Gull Lake Road.

We all arrived at the appointed place at the same time. I liked the white-haired Mr. Blue at first sight, and gave him a hearty handshake.

"My apologies for making you come all the way down the mountain," he said.

"Sir, I've been expecting you all summer, so I'm really pleased to meet you."

He introduced me to Mr. McEdwards, and then explained why they didn't climb the mountain.

"My time is limited this morning because we have to catch the noon train. Mr. Collier has been kind enough to be our guide today."

"Then you are excused from climbing Mount Electra, but I would have liked to have shown you the view."

"You call it Mount Electra, but at the district office we know it as Rock Lake Mountain."

Mr. Collier intervened and explained that the Webbs renamed all the mountains in the park when the family bought the property in the 1890s. "Electra was one of the ladies in the Webb family. In fact she was the wife of J. Watson Webb."

We spent a quarter of an hour together and I answered questions and told them about my work, and this made up somewhat for Mr. Blue not climbing the tower.

A few days later with September drawing to a close, I would long remember one last perfect day on the mountain. The glory of the fall season was all around me. Without a cloud in the sky, radiant sunshine spread over the countryside with a warm glow. Not a breeze ruffled the mirror-like surfaces of any pond or lake I could see.

I gazed southeast over the great spruces that marked the edge of a high cliff a couple of hundred feet below me. How splendid they looked silhouetted against the colorful valley nearly a mile away. Wild and vast, the beautiful carpet of trees in the valley enclosed the sparkling blue water of Rock Lake in gem-like beauty. Never again, I thought, would I see such a scene.

A week after Howard left, I began to expect a letter from him. When it finally came, with the Langley Field postmark, I knew he was safely back at the base. I enjoyed his letter until I read the last paragraph. He wrote, "I'll be going to another airfield soon and from there, we'll leave for overseas. That's all I can tell you, so if you don't hear from me for a couple weeks, I'll be on my way."

Slowly I reread his letter and realized I should have expected this. My prayers would be with him. But at the tower the next day, I had other things to think about. I would be leaving my mountain outpost soon and I began to feel anxious about the future. I was concerned about the direction my career would take. It wasn't easy to come to a decision, for I loved the out-of-doors. Yet, I knew that my parents had spent a considerable amount of money to give me an art education. I felt an obligation to put that training to work. Then, too, my sister Ann was working in Schenectady, and if I obtained work there or in Albany, we would be near each other. That was a comforting thought. By the time I reached the bottom of the mountain trail that afternoon, I had made up my mind. I would try for an art career in Albany.

My last day on the mountain was the coldest I had yet experienced. I was glad to be dressed warmly. In the tower room, the thermometer registered exactly forty degrees. All morning I saw nothing but closely packed gray clouds pushed by a steady west wind. Even my heavy jacket did not keep me warm, so I was glad for the need to make a couple of trips down the mountain.

I had a considerable load to carry on each descent of that well-known trail. In addition to some personal items, maps, and magazines, I had my archery set and the binoculars. Later, Mr. Collier would pick up the circular map under glass on the table, and fasten the windows securely so they wouldn't be worked loose by winter storms.

Before descending the tower for the last time, I took one last look at the familiar views. Then the sun broke through the clouds.

A section of the landscape filled with golden radiance for a fleeting moment. The sky brightened as the wind parted the clouds and suddenly, as I looked, spellbound, long rays of sunlight played like giant searchlights into Green Valley far below. It seemed like I was being given a mighty farewell salute from the heavens.

It was such a poignant moment that I could not leave. I waited a little longer, hoping the clouds would break up. The sky brightened and the subdued colors of the landscape came to life when the magic sunlight passed over them. The clouds dispersed gradually and a grand panorama of blended colors appeared, extending up one ridge and over another, one that faded to a soft violet on the far-off mountains.

I was elated that I had been at the tower long enough to see fall come into its own. I lowered the trap door behind me and descended the steps. As I made my way down the trail, I realized that I had come to know one of the grandest sights in the Adirondacks—the view from a fire tower.

Later, as I thought about it, I realized that my experiences as a fire tower observer taught me self-reliance, and gave me a greater appreciation of the Adirondacks. A love of these mountains has stayed with me to this day.

The winter after my stint in the tower, I left the Adirondacks for a short career as fashion illustrator for the Albany Times-Union. I lived and worked in Albany until 1946, but missed being in the mountains so much that I joined the local chapter of the Adirondack Mountain Club. Our frequent hikes into the Adirondacks eased some of my longing for the mountains I had come to love.

After the war, Howard and I were married and we settled in the Village of Long Lake, close to the center of the Adirondack Park. We had both come home to stay.

About the Author

Frances Boone Seaman is a lifelong resident of Long Lake. She and her husband, Howard, ran a contracting business there until 1986. She has been a part-time artist and is the former Long Lake Town Historian.